TIME TO SCRAP

KATHY FESMIRE

MEMORY MAKERS BOOKS

CINCINNATI, OHIO

WWW.MYCRAFTIVITY.COM

TIME TO SCRAP. Copyright © 2009 by Kathy Fesmire. Manufactured in China. All rights reserved. It is permissible for the purchaser to make the projects contained herein and sell them at fairs, bazaars and craft shows. No other part of this book may be reproduced in any form or by any electronic or mechanical means including information storage and retrieval systems without permission in writing from the publisher, except by a reviewer, who may quote a brief passage in review. Published by Memory Makers Books, an imprint of F+W Media, Inc., 4700 East Galbraith Road, Cincinnati, Ohio 45236. (800) 289-0963. First edition.

13 12 11 10 09   5 4 3 2 1

Distributed in Canada by Fraser Direct
100 Armstrong Avenue
Georgetown, ON, Canada L7G 5S4
Tel: (905) 877-4411

Distributed in the U.K. and Europe by David & Charles
Brunel House, Newton Abbot, Devon, TQ12 4PU, England
Tel: (+44) 1626 323200, Fax: (+44) 1626 323319
E-mail: postmaster@davidandcharles.co.uk

Distributed in Australia by Capricorn Link
P.O. Box 704, S. Windsor, NSW 2756 Australia
Tel: (02) 4577-3555

Library of Congress Cataloging-in-Publication Data
Fesmire, Kathy.
  Time to scrap : techniques for fast, fun and fabulous scrapbook layouts / by Kathy Fesmire.
    p. cm.
  Includes index.
  ISBN-13: 978-1-59963-083-0 (pbk. : alk. paper)
  ISBN-10: 1-59963-083-4 (pbk. : alk. paper)
  1. Photograph albums. 2. Scrapbooking. I. Title.
  TR501.F478 2009
  745.593--dc22
                    2009015108

www.fwmedia.com

About the Author

Kathy is an art teacher and scrapbooking instructor who not only loves to scrapbook herself, but also finds great joy in inspiring others to scrap. When she is not writing and scrapping, she spends her time running around delivering three of her four children to numerous places and events. (One can drive herself!) A 2004 Memory Makers Master, she teaches at numerous scrapbook conventions across the nation. Her work has appeared in many recent Memory Makers books, including all three *Ask the Masters* books, *Type Cast*, *Toddlerhood*, *Scrapbooking the School Years* and *601 Great Scrapbook Ideas*.

EDITOR: LIZ CASLER
DESIGNER: KELLY O'DELL
PRODUCTION COORDINATOR: GREG NOCK
COVER ILLUSTRATION AND INTERIOR ILLUSTRATIONS:
    LISA BALLARD, SCOTT HULL ASSOCIATES
PHOTOGRAPHER: ADAM HAND

METRIC CONVERSION CHART

TO CONVERT	TO	MULTIPLY BY
Inches	Centimeters	2.54
Centimeters	Inches	0.4
Feet	Centimeters	30.5
Centimeters	Feet	0.03
Yards	Meters	0.9
Meters	Yards	1.1

DEDICATION

I can't imagine scrapping without my four favorite subjects—Alex, Morgan, Hayden and Isaac. You are a constant source of joy, and you make me laugh every single day. I feel so blessed and lucky to have you guys in my life. Thanks for putting up with my absence, the frozen dinners, frantic moments and all the modeling for pictures that you had to do while I was writing this book. I love all of you with all my heart.

ACKNOWLEDGMENTS

To my whole family, thanks for being my inspiration and my support. You guys are the best. To my mom and dad, thanks for babysitting and picking up and dropping off the kids numerous times because I was busy. I couldn't have done it without you.

To my husband, Austin, thank you for all the times you did the tuck-ins, the dishes and the laundry so I could write this book. You kept the Diet Coke stocked, and you make a mean frozen pizza.

To my scrapbooking buddies, Deb, Nan, Karen and Patti (in no particular order because I love them all the same). Thank you for being cheerleaders, idea bouncer-off-ers, people to bum things off of and, most of all, a huge source of laughter and love. My love of scrapbooking comes from our weekends away scrapping, laughing and watching *Diary of a Mad Black Woman* countless times. Thank you, thank you, thank you!

Thanks to my parents and Deb, Nan and Alana for the use of your incredible pictures.

A special thank you to Jennifer, Julie, Shaunte and Shannon for your unbelievable contributions to this book. Every layout you did was amazing. You all rock.

A big thank you to the entire Memory Makers Books staff. You made being a first-time author much less scary than I thought it was going to be.

To all of my other friends and family, thank you for your support, your encouragement and your inspiration. I am forever grateful. Love you!

TABLE OF CONTENTS

INTRODUCTION

How many times have you heard non-scrappers say, "I just don't have the time to scrapbook"? I have felt that way myself many times, but scrapbooking is so much more than just a hobby or a means of preserving memories to me. It is my creative outlet and my method of self-expression, so I make time for it as often as I can.

When I first started scrapbooking, I labored over my pages for an exorbitant amount of time, piling on the products and making sure every detail was attended to. (What was I thinking?!) But as the years went by, my family and my responsibilities grew while my time to scrapbook shrank. No more five-hour layouts for me! I needed to find a way to speed up my work without losing my creativity or the joy I found in scrapbooking.

I began to look for ways to use more photos and fewer products and to pull everything together quickly while still creating pages I could be proud of. This simple idea became the topic for a convention class, which in turn inspired this book. Let's face it, we all are busy. Let me give you a hand with a book full of time-saving ideas, fun techniques, frugal suggestions and fabulous multiphoto page designs.

Fast, fun, frugal and fabulous layouts are spelled out for you on the pages of this book. Every layout holds at least three photos so you can make the most of each page. In addition, each layout is labeled with the estimated time it will take to complete once you have gathered your supplies, so you will know exactly how much scrap time to plan for. With 30 step-out techniques and extra tips, you are sure to take away ideas from each and every layout. So don't sweat it, pick a layout, a technique or a sketch, and have fun!

Let me help you find Time to Scrap!
KATHY

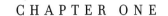

CHAPTER ONE

Fast

Just like the rabbit in *Alice in Wonderland*, I am constantly on the verge of being late for a very important date! So time is a valuable commodity to me. As my life got busier, it was harder and harder to find time to scrapbook, and that had to change. I spent so much time on each page that I never had time to complete one. I had to change my mind-set about what made a good scrapbook page and how much time I was willing to devote to each one.

I told myself, "No more than 90 minutes on anything." Then I challenged myself to create a great page in an hour...then 30 minutes...then 15. Guess what? I still loved them, even without the tons of products and painstaking techniques that took hours to do. This chapter is all about the ideas I discovered while I was challenging myself to speed things up. Whether you have 15 minutes or 90 minutes you will find layouts and techniques in this chapter to meet your needs. Turn the page to find some great time-saving ideas.

STITCHING WITHOUT THE machine

I love the look of stitching on my pages but don't want to drag out my sewing machine every time I want to create this fantastic look. Try these techniques to get the look of stitching without the hassle.

30–45 MINUTES

STITCH WITH A PERFORATING TOOL

My daughter cracks me up with these gloves on while she carves her pumpkin. I just had to make a page celebrating her little quirk. Once the basics of the layout were put together, I knew the white band of journaling needed some extra pop. To create the look of stitching, I used my perforating tool. This is one of the fastest ways to get the look of stitching, and it added just the extra something that this layout needed.

Supplies

Cardstock; patterned paper (BasicGrey); chipboard elements, letters, button, ribbons (American Crafts); stamp (Studio G); alphabet stickers (Making Memories); flower (Prima); perforating tool (EK Success); Misc: ink, buttons, staples

MATERIALS
INK PAD,
PERFORATING TOOL

1 Roll your perforating tool over the ink pad several times to cover the blade.

2 Roll the tool over your paper to achieve the look of stitching. Reload the tool with ink as needed.

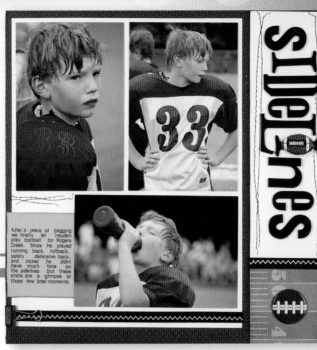

ADD RUB-ON STITCHING

Stitching on photos can be scary because it risks messing up the page or tearing the photos. I love these pictures of my kids on the pier so much that I didn't want to take any chances, and I certainly didn't want to have to reprint the pictures and redo my layout! A quick and far less frightening alternative is to use rub-on stitching. They can be cut into pieces and placed directly on your photos. This zigzag pattern looks great as photo corners that add dimension to the layout without adding bulk.

Supplies

Cardstock; patterned paper (We R Memory Keepers, Sassafras Lass, Reminisce, Scenic Route); chipboard ring and sun (Creek Bank Creations); rub-on stitching (K&Company); alphabet stickers (American Crafts); ribbon (Offray); Misc: pen, ink, circle punch

STITCH WITH A PAPER PIERCER AND PEN

These photos that my husband took of my son were so amazing I wanted to make sure that nothing I added to the layout distracted from them. This straight stitching was so simple to do and made a big impact in a small amount of time. I love overlapping the lines of "stitching" to create this casual look. The added "thread" at the ends gives it a real machine-stitched feel.

Supplies

Cardstock (Bazzill Basics, Paperbilities); patterned paper (BoBunny, Karen Foster Design); chipboard letters (Heidi Swapp); football accent, brad (Karen Foster Design); paper piercing tool (EK Success); binder clip (Li'l Davis Designs); zigzag border (Doodlebug Design); ribbon (The Paper Studio); Misc: pen, ink

30-45 MINUTES

30-45 MINUTES

MATERIALS
PAPER PIERCING TOOL, MICRON PEN

1 Roll the paper piercing tool over the paper.

2 Pull the pen between the holes, stopping at each hole. Use the pen to draw a "thread" at each end.

USE ACRYLIC PAINT TO SPEED THINGS UP

Paint can be a quick and easy accent. Try the following techniques to cut down on your work time.

PAINT EDGES OF PHOTOS

Matting photos can be time-consuming, so try painting the edges of your photos instead to speed things along. By alternating black and white paint on the edges, I created contrast between photos that all have similar tones. The simple accents and title created from stickers made quick work of this family layout. Using numbers from different sticker sheets gives the number line more interest. The number six was highlighted by using a different color, matting it and framing it with a slide mount. Save yourself some time by breaking out the paint for your photos.

Make It Fast!

Crop pictures, check for placement and paint the photo edges before putting together the page elements. This allows time for the paint to dry while you work.

Supplies

Cardstock; patterned paper (My Mind's Eye); alphabet stickers (Karen Foster Design); number stickers (American Crafts, Karen Foster Design); slide mount (Keller's Creations); ribbon (Offray); Misc: staples, acrylic paint

USE PAINT TO CREATE A MAT

These beach pictures were perfect for this quick and easy painted-mat technique. To achieve this look, place your photos on the page and trace around them with a pencil. Put a small amount of paint on a foam brush and lightly drag it over and just outside your pencil lines. Let the paint dry and then adhere your photos for a soft, simple look. This saves the time you would have spent matting your photos and allows you to use any color of paint that matches your layout.

Supplies

Patterned paper (Imaginisce, BasicGrey); chipboard letters (EK Success); chipboard accent (Miss Elizabeth's); chipboard tag numbers (Creek Bank Creations); stamps (Art Warehouse); rub-ons (Fancy Pants Designs); ribbon (American Crafts); Misc: ink

PAINT A QUICK SWIRL

Are you afraid of painting on your pages? Don't be! It's fast and easy, and the best part is you can paint any shape in any color to match whatever subject you have. This page with its blue-eyed angel just screamed for some swirls. To make sure I liked the placement before I committed to the paint, I used a pencil to draw light lines that I could follow with the paintbrush. To create this look, use a thin brush and let your hand go freely as you move the paint over the page. Don't worry if it isn't perfect. This accent is supposed to look hand-painted. Dress up the painted swirls with flowers, rhinestones and a gel pen for highlights.

Supplies

Cardstock; patterned paper (Daisy D's, Karen Foster Design); chipboard ring (EK Success); chipboard letters, rhinestones (Heidi Swapp); flowers (American Crafts); ribbon (Crafts, Etc!); flower brads (Karen Foster Design); pen (Uni-ball); Misc: buttons

45-60 MINUTES

Make It Fabulous!

Try printing your focal photo in color and your supporting photos in black and white to draw special attention to the subject.

Transform Transparencies

Try these techniques to customize transparencies to make quick custom embellishments.

sweet

Morgan is such a sweet and beautiful girl! So many people come to me and tell me what a kind heart she has, what a good person she is and how sweet she is. It is so nice to know that we have raised a young lady who is just as pretty on the inside as she is on the outside.

May 05

30-45 MINUTES

CREATE A CUSTOM TRANSPARENCY

On this day when my daughter won a Citizenship Award, she was particularly sweet. (Other days, not so much!) She looked so feminine and pretty that I wanted to create a totally girly layout. I love this flower punch but wanted the accent to be more substantial, so I used the punch to create a custom transparency. The outline and brad centers were just the extra something that these flower punches needed to increase the girl factor of this layout!

Supplies

Cardstock; patterned paper (My Mind's Eye); sticker letters (American Crafts); brads (The Paper Studio, Karen Foster Design); month sticker (Karen Foster Design); ribbon (The Paper Studio, Michaels); Misc: flower punch

materials

FLOWER PUNCH, CARDSTOCK, TRANSPARENCY, PERMANENT MARKER, DECORATIVE BRADS

1 Punch the shape from heavyweight cardstock.

2 Place the punched shape on a transparency and trace with your pen. Freehand draw a second image around the first. Create a grouping of shapes if desired.

3 Adhere the punched shapes to your page and overlay the transparency, matching the traced images. Adhere the transparency to the paper using brads as flower centers.

PRINT A TRANSPARENCY FOR A DRAMATIC EMBELLISHMENT

Need a very specific embellishment? Create it yourself with a transparency and your printer. I couldn't wait to make this page of my son with his 100 tattoos and tried to find some way to add the numbers 1–100, but every option I found was going to be way too large and take way too long. So I pulled out a transparency, hopped on the computer and typed out the numbers in the font and size I wanted. To help the numbers stand out from the patterned paper background, I painted the back of the transparency with acrylic paint.

Supplies

Patterned paper (The Paper Loft, BasicGrey, Scenic Route); chipboard alphabet and numbers (Heidi Swapp); rub-ons (Making Memories, K&Company); stamps (Autumn Leaves, The Paper Studio); transparency (3M); ribbon (Offray); Misc: staples, ink, acrylic paint

45–60 MINUTES

Make It Fabulous!

Use this same idea for printing specific words or images. Internet clip art sites are a great resource for images, and many don't cost a dime!

EASY TITLE PLACEMENT

Trying to line up the letters in your title sometimes can be difficult to manage. Try these great techniques for easy title placement every time!

PAGE BY SHAUNTE WADLEY

45-60 MINUTES

USE A CIRCLE TO PLACE YOUR TITLE

After adding a cardstock border, Shaunte felt her layout was looking rather boxy. To break up the rigid feel, she added some curves by placing her title in a circle and adding a ring to the page. To make sure the title stays in a perfect circle, use a large circle as a placement guide. The curves she created softened up the layout nicely.

Supplies

Cardstock; patterned paper (BoBunny); chipboard (Polar Bear Press); brads (Karen Foster Design); die cut alphabet (QuicKutz)

~~~) *Make It Fabulous!*

You can add stability to a thin patterned paper background by adding a cardstock border all the way around the page like Shaunte did.

MATERIALS

CARDSTOCK, CIRCLE CUTTER, DIE CUT ALPHABET

1 Cut a ring from cardstock with a circle cutter.

2 Place the circle from the center of the ring on the page. Adhere the title around the circle.

3 Remove the circle and add the ring to the page, trimming and securing it under the first and last letters of the title.

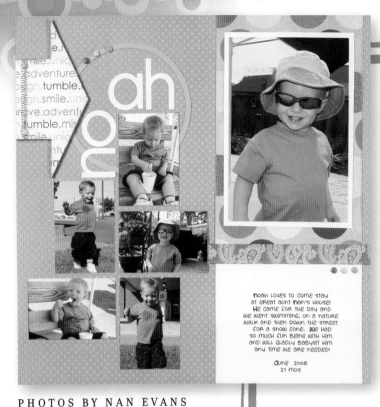

PHOTOS BY NAN EVANS

FOLLOW THE LINE OF THE PHOTOS FOR EASY TITLE PLACEMENT

Trying to place sticker letters in a straight line can be frustrating and time-consuming. Using your photos to guide your letter placement not only can save you time but can also keep you from pulling your hair out. Don't feel like you have to keep your title in a straight line. I wrapped the title around the corner of the photo for a simple but interesting effect.

Supplies

Cardstock; patterned paper (BoBunny, My Mind's Eye); chipboard arrow (Creek Bank Creations); sticker alphabet (American Crafts); rub-ons (K&Company); ribbon (Offray); brads (Karen Foster Design); Misc: ink

 *Make It Fabulous!*

Did you know that people's eyes are drawn to the upper right-hand corner when they look at things? This makes it the perfect spot for the focal photo on your pages.

CREATE A WHIMSICAL TITLE

Sometimes the fastest way to place your title is to not align any letters! When I saw these colorful pictures from the candy store, I knew this layout would be a great way to use lots of leftover stickers for a title and journaling. Because the letters were different shapes and sizes, I purposely varied my height placement for a casual look. Not only was this title quick to complete, it helped clean out my leftover sticker stash!

Supplies

Cardstock; patterned paper (Scenic Route); rub-ons (K&Company); alphabet stickers (American Crafts, EK Success, Karen Foster Design); ribbon (Offray)

use pre-made embellishments

Pre-made embellishments can save you time and effort. Use them as is or add your own touch to them.

USE A DRAMATIC EMBELLISHMENT

Using one large, premade accent on a page not only creates impact but also saves time by eliminating the need for other embellishments. This eye-catching, beaded frog is a floral department find from a local craft store. When I saw it, I knew it was the perfect embellishment for photos of my youngest son hopping on the trampoline. The green, scalloped border is reminiscent of a lily pad and provides the perfect resting place for this glitzy amphibian. Subtle patterns and a simple color scheme enhance the photos without competing with the frog embellishment. Be on the lookout for oversized embellishments to make a statement on your scrapbook pages and to cut down on your work time.

Supplies

Patterned paper (EK Success, The Paper Studio); beaded frog (Hobby Lobby); alphabet stickers (Chartwell Studio, American Crafts); chipboard alphabet (Heidi Swapp); ribbon (American Crafts, Offray); ric rack (Queen & Co.); Misc: acrylic paint

15-30 MINUTES

Make It Fabulous!

Position a large, single embellishment facing your photos to direct the viewer's eye toward the focus of the page.

backyard

gaRDen

Mom and dad always have such gorgeous flowers in their garden. These bright pink lilies and gladiolas are some of my favorite flowers.

Summer 2008

30-45 MINUTES

PHOTOS BY PAUL KETRON

MODIFY PRE-MADE EMBELLISHMENTS

I would never take the time to cut out and stitch this pretty flower embellishment, but then again, I didn't have to! The work was already done for me in this felt flower gift tag, which I loved, but it had a bright blue center that just didn't work. I simply added a silk flower and button to match my color scheme and to dress it up a bit. It made the perfect embellishment for this garden page, added texture and dimension, and only took about two minutes to alter.

Supplies

Cardstock; patterned paper (BoBunny); felt flower accent (Hallmark); silk flowers (Teters); chipboard alphabet (Heidi Swapp); ribbon (Offray); Misc: buttons, ink

ADD SOME QUICK SPARKLE TO YOUR PAGES!

Who doesn't like a little bling every once in a while? Check out these quick and easy ideas for adding some glam to your pages.

PHOTOS BY ALANA TURNER

CREATE A QUICK LINE OF EMBELLISHMENTS WITH LEFTOVER BRADS AND BUTTONS

I always have a few brads and buttons from collections left after using them on the initial page I purchase them for. Creating this page gave me an opportunity to pull from my stash of leftovers and make a whimsical diagonal accent that came together super quickly. After applying the rub-on stitching, I used it as a guide for the placement of all the brads and buttons.

Supplies

Cardstock; patterned paper (Imaginisce, DCWV); chipboard alphabet (American Crafts); brads (Karen Foster Design); flower buttons (Favorite Findings); rub-ons (DCWV); white pen (Uni-ball); Misc: buttons, ink, scallop punch

Make It Fabulous!

When you have a layout with strong horizontal and vertical lines (created by the photos in this layout), try adding a diagonal line of embellishments to soften the look of the page.

SPRAY GLITTER FOR QUICK AND EASY GLAM

PHOTOS BY ALANA TURNER

The holidays always make me think of sparkle and glitter. I wanted to create a poinsettia accent that would shine just like the glitter-laden title. I drew out the petals on red paper first and then gave it a quick mist of spray glitter. After a short, 10-minute dry time, I cut out my petals, inked the edges and adhered them to the page. Then I added beads as the flower center for a little extra sparkle. This is a quick way to add some glam to a page and can be used to dress up any accent for any theme.

45–60 MINUTES

Supplies

Patterned paper (Cosmo Cricket); precut scalloped circle (Keller's Creations cut from Sweetwater); spray glitter (FloraCraft); chipboard alphabet (Wal-Mart); alphabet and number stickers (Making Memories); beads (Sulyn Industries); ribbon (The Paper Studio); Misc: ink

ATTACH IN A SNAP

Adhesive isn't the only way to attach elements to your page. Try these quick methods of attaching everything from photos to embellishments onto scrapbook pages.

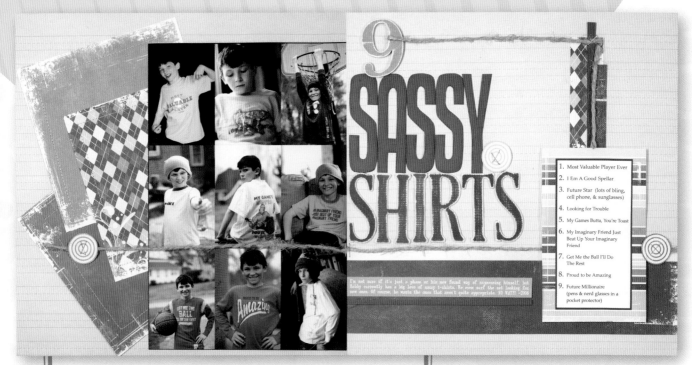

PAGE BY SHANNON TAYLOR

STAPLE PAGE ELEMENTS TO YOUR LAYOUT

Shannon's layout about her son's love of graphic shirts came together in a snap by stapling elements to the page. Thin items, like the hemp Shannon used, are often difficult to adhere without any adhesive showing and can be a major pain to attach. By stapling the hemp in place, Shannon not only saved herself time but also kept her layout neat and tidy.

Supplies

Patterned papers (Karen Foster Design, We R Memory Keepers, Teresa Collins); alphabet and numeric chipboard (BasicGrey, Pressed Petals); hemp rope (Magic Scraps); Misc: staples; fonts: Webster, Palotino Linotype

45-60 MINUTES

Make It Fabulous!

Use an element that runs across both pages of a double-page layout, like the hemp Shannon used, to draw the viewer's eyes from one page to the next.

PAGE BY SHAUNTE WADLEY

ATTACH PHOTOS WITH PAPER CLIPS

Shaunte printed the individual photos of her kids in wallet size, intending to fit them all on one layout with the group photo. They got lost on the page, so she created the squares to mat them with. Then the photos seemed boring, just hanging out on the squares, so she picked up these colorful paper clips from the dollar store to match the striped paper. They are a perfect accent to the layout, and at a dollar a box, you can't beat the price! She used the paper clips to adhere the photos but added a small glue dot under each photo to make sure they were securely attached.

Supplies

Cardstock; patterned paper (BoBunny); paper clips (Greenbrier International); brads (All Stuck Up, BoBunny); foam alphabet (American Crafts)

PAGE BY JEN GALLACHER

HOLD EMBELLISHMENTS WITH BINDER CLIPS

Jen wanted some texture to go with her black, white and orange theme, so she added twine to the layout. To add dimension, she used foam tape under the orange border and then attached the office clips. She laced twine through the office clips several times and then tied charms to the thread before knotting it. This is a really quick way to thread twine, and it adds a cool look to the layout as well.

Supplies

Cardstock; patterned paper (SEI); twine (Craft Supply); charms, black mini brads (Karen Foster Design); chipboard, chipboard circle (Scenic Route); embossing folder, die cut machine (Cuttlebug for Provo Craft); letter stickers (Doodlebug Design); Misc: binder clips, pinking scissors; font: 2Peas Tubby

speedy journaling ideas

Journaling is usually left until last—often put off until another day. These simple journaling ideas will help you bite the bullet and do your journaling in a snap.

materials

ENVELOPE, PEN, PAPER TRIMMER

HIDE JOURNALING IN AN ENVELOPE

Hidden journaling is a great way to tell a story while still using the maximum number of photos, but raising the photos from the page to accommodate the moving journaling block and trying to find ways to keep the hidden journaling in place can be a challenge. This envelope trick is the fastest way I have found to create hidden journaling. The journaling remains in place and slides easily in and out of the envelope without having to raise the photos off the page.

Supplies

Patterned paper, brads, rub-ons, chipboard alphabet (BasicGrey); rub-on borders (The Paper Studio); rhinestones (Darice); Misc: tab punch, staples, acrylic paint, ink

45–60 MINUTES

1 Seal an envelope and place your journaling tag at the bottom of the envelope, marking where the tag will extend above the photo.

2 Cut the envelope where marked with a paper trimmer.

3 Adhere the envelope to the back of the photo mat; then adhere the mat to your page and slide the tag into the envelope.

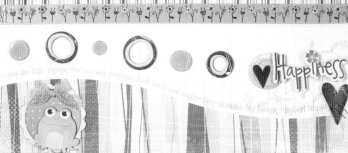

15-30 MINUTES

USE A PREPRINTED QUOTE AS YOUR JOURNALING

Ever been at a loss for words? Many companies feel your pain and have provided patterned papers with preprinted quotes. By adding a few simple embellishments, a premade title and three gorgeous pictures, I was able to complete this layout literally in minutes!

Supplies

Cardstock; patterned paper, chipboard accessories and title (Fancy Pants Designs); scalloped circle (The Paper Studio); ribbon (Michaels, Offray); Misc: circle punches, staples

Make It Frugal!

Don't overlook embellishments just because they might not seem to coordinate at first glance. This chipboard frog might not have worked on its own with the girly photos, but by simply adding a ribbon bow to its head, it is the perfect touch! Look for ways to alter the embellishments you have to stretch your scrapbooking buck.

COMBINE YOUR PHOTO MATS AND JOURNALING

I love being able to include numerous photos on each page. It saves time and helps capture the event I am scrapbooking. But I get tired of cutting mats for multiple photos. Try this fast trick. Print your journaling in the middle of a sheet of white paper, adhere your photos around the journaling and trim the paper evenly. Four cuts and you have quickly matted all four photos.

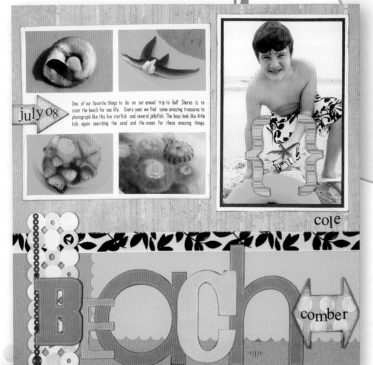

30-45 MINUTES

Supplies

Cardstock; scalloped paper (DCWV); patterned paper (Miss Elizabeth's); die cut letters, brackets (Colorbök); chipboard arrows (Creek Bank Creations); chipboard circles (Fancy Pants Designs); rub-ons (The Paper Studio); ribbon (Michaels); circle paper border (Doodlebug Design); Misc: ink

surround your focal point TO HIGHLIGHT

Nothing makes a focal point stand out like surrounding it.
Try these simple ideas to help your subject stand out on your page

happy birthday delicate butterfly

I have to say that seeing Ms. anna Banana running around in a tutu & fairy wings on Her 1st Birthday Just about made my year!

DATE: 10/07

30-45
MINUTES

CREATE A PHOTO MAT WITH A PREMADE SCALLOPED BORDER

Don't you just love the look of this long, tall photo? Shannon used the edges of scalloped cardstock as a mat by simply cutting the outside edges of the paper and placing the pieces down the long sides of the oversized photo. The large scallop was perfect for such a big picture, but this technique can be used with smaller scallops and smaller photos as well. If you would like the scalloped mat to go all the way around the photo, simply match the scallops and miter the corners with a ruler and craft knife.

Supplies

Patterned paper, blue scalloped paper, ribbon, brads, letter sticker, date sticker (American Crafts); white scalloped paper (Bazzill Basics); wire (Artistic Wire); Misc: foam adhesive; font: Cherub

PAGE BY
SHANNON TAYLOR

Cole is growing up and doesn't really want to be the subject of all my photography. In fact it's hard to get him to let me take his picture at all. This day, at his grandparents, I caught him playing around in a tree and got my camera out. For the first time in a long time he let me take these shots without complaining and he even smiled!

30-45 MINUTES

FILL THE PAGE WITH LARGE PHOTOS

PHOTOS BY NAN EVANS

When I got these gorgeous photos from my friend, I was planning on trimming down the large photo so other elements would fit on the page without overlapping it. But once I laid it out on the page, I knew that leaving the photo full sized would speed things along by eliminating the need for a lot of paper and embellishments. Because the largest photo had lots of space around the perimeter, I overlapped the smaller photos without taking away from the subject of the large photo.

Supplies

Patterned paper (Fancy Pants Designs, The Paper Loft); scalloped paper (DCWV); chipboard elements (Fancy Pants Designs, Sassafras Lass); chipboard letters (EK Success); rub-ons (Fancy Pants Designs); precut ring (Keller's Creations); ribbon (American Crafts, Offray); Misc: ink

Make It Fabulous!

To highlight a subject in a large photo, try placing a neutral-colored cardstock or chipboard ring on the photo around the focal point.

CHAPTER TWO

Fun

Don't you just love learning something new? I always enjoy trying new techniques or new twists on old ones. However, if something has too many steps or takes a huge amount of time, I usually give up on it before I am finished or skip it entirely. With my newfound attitude of more photos, less time, more fun, I had to come up with some really cool techniques that weren't too complicated.

In this chapter you will find new uses for products you have on hand, as well as techniques that use some products you may never have tried before. Some of the techniques literally take 2 minutes, others a bit longer. Even the longer techniques take no more than 90 minutes to complete. No matter how much time you have to scrapbook, you can try the techniques in this chapter. Challenge yourself to try a technique that is new to you and remember to have fun!

MODELING PASTE TECHNIQUES

Modeling paste is a fun and unique medium to work with. Try these quick techniques to add interest and texture to your pages.

PHOTOS BY ALANA TURNER

45-60 MINUTES

MASK A TITLE WITH MODELING PASTE AND CHIPBOARD LETTERS

What is it about mud that just screams "jump in" to kids? Not only did my sons not mind being muddy, but they actually rubbed mud all over themselves! When I saw these photos, I knew I wanted to create that gooey, dirty look on my page. Masking a title with modeling paste over chipboard letters created exactly the look I was going for. I emphasized the title by adhering the chipboard letters covered with modeling paste below the masked title.

Supplies

Cardstock; patterned paper and stickers (BasicGrey); number stickers (American Crafts); alphabet stickers, date stickers, micron pen (EK Success); chipboard letters (Heidi Swapp); modeling paste (Winsor & Newton); Misc: acrylic paint, ink, buttons, staples

MATERIALS

CHIPBOARD ALPHABET, ACRYLIC PAINT, MODELING PASTE, PAPER PLATE, SPREADING TOOL, TWEEZERS

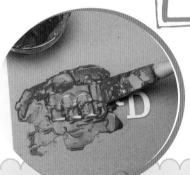

1 Place chipboard letters on your page, leaving room on all sides for modeling paste.

2 Stir the acrylic paint with the modeling paste until the desired color is achieved. Spread the modeling paste with a flat tool, covering your letters to the thickness of the chipboard.

3 Using tweezers, remove the letters and set aside. Adhere the letters to your page when the modeling paste is dry.

Oh the joy of finally having a little girl! (And she's a girly one at that!) Ashleigh loves to dress up, loves to have her picture made and loves everything that is glitzy, glammy and pink! That made our shopping trip and fashion shoot the perfect way for her to combine all her favorites and give me a chance to get some great pictures of her!

PHOTOS BY
ALANA TURNER

45–60
MINUTES

ADD TEXTURE WITH MAGIC MESH AND MODELING PASTE

I just love the soft, feminine look of these pink textured dots, and they were so easy to create! Place Magic Mesh on the background paper, holding the edges down firmly. (Do not remove the backing from the mesh.) Spread white modeling paste over the mesh using a flat tool and then remove the mesh. Let it dry for 10–15 minutes and then rub chalk ink gently over the top of the modeling paste dots. The dots provide texture and the pink chalk ink adds a light, feminine touch to the page.

Supplies

Cardstock; patterned paper, stickers (BasicGrey); brads (Karen Foster Design); crown brad (The Paper Studio); paper flowers (Target); felt flowers, ribbons (American Crafts); mesh (Magic Mesh); modeling paste (Winsor & Newton); Misc: tickets, acrylic paint, ink

Make It Fast!

Try placing your pages that have wet elements on them directly under your work light. The heat from the lamp will speed up the dry time.

DISTRESS YOUR ELEMENTS

You don't always have to take your products as they are. Distressing can give them a totally different look, and these techniques are an easy way to change up your scrapbook stash.

Boys are competitive...no matter what!

So even good friends can turn a

a fun day at the Pool into a

diving contest...scores and all!

August 2006

SCORE board

Make It Fabulous!

Boring background in your photos? Help your photo subjects stand out by framing them with thin strips of cardstock.

30–45 MINUTES

DISTRESS ACRYLIC LETTERS WITH PAINT

Looking at these pictures of my son and his friends having a diving contest makes me smile. We had such a fun day, and I wanted this layout to reflect that feeling. After choosing the colorful patterned papers, I wanted to create a standout title. Using lime green paint and this painting technique with acetate letters was the perfect choice. The beauty of this technique is that your title color choices are only limited to the countless shades of acrylic paint available, so it can be used with any theme or color palette.

Supplies

Cardstock; patterned paper, arrows, journaling block (Scenic Route); acrylic letters (Creek Bank Creations); metal brackets (Around the Block); alphabet and number stickers (American Crafts); precut rings (Keller's Creations cut from Piggy Tales); chalk ink (Clearsnap); Misc: acrylic paint

MATERIALS

FOAM PLATE, CLEAR ACETATE LETTERS, ACRYLIC PAINT, FOAM BRUSH, SANDPAPER, PAPER TOWEL

1 Paint the backs of the clear acetate letters with a foam brush and acrylic paint and allow them to dry completely.

2 Rub the paint gently using a fine-grit sandpaper to lightly remove some areas of paint.

3 Place the letters face down on a paper towel. Paint over the green paint with a foam brush and white acrylic paint. Let the letters dry before adhering them to the page.

oct '06

pumpkin farm

184524 184524 184523 184523

Isaac had such a great time at the Guthrie Pumpkin farm. Not only did he find the perfect pumpkin for his Jack-O-Lantern, he got to feed the calves and pet all kinds of farm animals. The day ended with a great time going through the hay maze and a picnic lunch. What a wonderful Fall field trip it was!

15-30 MINUTES

DISTRESS A TITLE BY TEARING AND SANDING ALPHABET STICKERS

I just love these pictures of Isaac at the pumpkin farm. He had such a great time. I wanted to create a rustic, distressed title to go with the farm pictures, and this sanding technique provided just the look this page needed. Sand the outside edges of the letters prior to removing them from the sticker sheet to prevent the sandpaper from damaging your background paper.

Supplies

Cardstock; patterned paper (The Paper Loft); alphabet stickers (American Crafts); wooden sign, brad (Karen Foster Design); tags (Avery); ribbon (Offray); Misc: tickets, sandpaper, ink

MATERIALS
ALPHABET STICKERS, SANDPAPER

1 Lightly sand the alphabet sticker edges while they are still on the backing.

2 Remove the stickers and tear each one at different angles.

3 Place the stickers on your page, matching the torn edges to each other. Gently sand the torn edges for emphasis.

STAMP YOUR HEART OUT

Stamps are such versatile tools and can be used with so many different media.
Try these fun and simple stamping techniques to add interest and texture to your pages.

PHOTOS BY NAN EVANS

STAMP AND LAYER TRANSPARENCIES

I don't know about you, but I am often reluctant to stamp on my background paper for fear I won't like it once it is done. I solved this problem by stamping on transparencies, which gave me the freedom to move the design around until I liked the way it looked. With a few well-placed brads holding the transparencies in place, I was able to see the entire design without ever having to put stamp to paper!

Supplies

Cardstock; patterned paper (Fancy Pants Designs); acrylic stamps, tag (Keller's Creations); rubber stamp (Stampabilities); alphabet stickers, chipboard numbers and scroll, felt flowers, ribbon (American Crafts); paper flowers (Prima); brads (Karen Foster Design); Misc: acrylic paint, ink, buttons, scalloped circle punch

45-60 MINUTES

MATERIALS
StazOn ink, stamps, transparencies

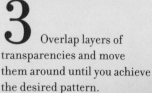

1
Using StazOn ink, stamp the background pattern on a transparency.

2
Stamp your second and third patterns on separate transparencies.

3
Overlap layers of transparencies and move them around until you achieve the desired pattern.

On a trip to Europe we spent some time in Aberfeldy, Scotland. On a hiking trail through Weems Woods we found these gorgeous carvings in the trees that had fallen over or been broken off and we just had to get pictures of them. The simple mushroom is just as impressive as the intricate carving of the mythical figure and the dragon. What gorgeous artwork to find along a trail.

Weems Woods

October 2007

DESTINATION
VACATION
RECREATION

60–90 MINUTES

PHOTOS BY PAUL KETRON

STAMP AND CUT OUT A TITLE

When I saw this cardboard donut in the bottom of a box, I snatched it up and stuck it in my "to use" stash in my scrapbooking room. I love the way it looks; it is a perfect rustic background for this stamped title technique. After stamping with ink on cardstock, I traced around the stamped letters with a micron pen and then cut them out with sharp scissors. Simple accents like buttons and rustic wooden embellishments are all that are needed to enhance these amazing photos.

Supplies

Cardstock; patterned paper (BasicGrey, The Paper Studio); stamps (Magnetic Poetry); wooden accents (Go West Studios); corduroy and leaf buttons (Junkits); micron pen (EK Success); Misc: ink, cardboard ring, punches

Make It Fast!

A quick and easy alternative to matting photos is to gently sand the edges with an emery board. I keep one in my tool jar to give subtle definition to the edges of my photos

STAMP A TEXTURED TITLE   PAGE BY JULIE JOHNSON

New York, New York—the city so nice they named it twice! What fantastic pictures of some of the amazing sights in the city! The vertical placement of the photos and title, even the title itself, all convey the same sense of awe that Julie felt in the city that day looking up at the sights. She created an amazing treatment to use on her title to add texture and shine. The look and mood of this technique can be changed to fit any theme by changing stamp images or ink, paint or pen colors.

Supplies

Cardstock; patterned paper (Karen Foster Design); chipboard letters (Everlasting Keepsakes); "the city" stickers (Me & My Big Ideas); Magic Texture paint (Delta Creative); stamps (Hero Arts); paint pen, fixative (Krylon); chalk ink (Clearsnap); word stickers (EK Success); rub-ons (BasicGrey)

60–90 MINUTES

materials

CHIPBOARD LETTERS, MAGIC TEXTURE PAINT, BABY WIPES, RUBBER STAMP, CHALK INK, SILVER PAINT PEN, WORKABLE FIXATIVE

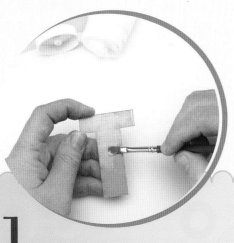

1 Coat a chipboard letter with Magic Texture paint and let it set for 1 minute.

2 Wipe your stamp with a baby wipe and stamp into the textured paint. Repeat the process until the desired pattern is achieved and let it set for 15 minutes.

3 Lightly rub the letter with ink until the desired color is achieved. (Be careful not to ink into the stamp pattern.)

4 Run a silver pen lightly over the inked letter.

5 Seal with workable fixative. (Fixative is required for the letter to dry properly.)

08 *March*

Smile

CARNIVAL *fun*

Cozumel

Morgan and I had a great time on this cruise to Cozumel. Just the two of us went for work but we got to do tons of fun things including an excursion of a dune buggy ride and snorkeling trip once we docked in Cozumel. Hopefully we will get to take more vacations just the two of us.

CREATE REVERSE-STAMP EMBELLISHMENTS

I love the texture that acrylic stamps can create, and they are not limited to use with ink! This reverse stamp technique is done with acrylic paint and has a totally different look than stamping with ink. While stamping with ink can add visual texture, physically it is flat and two dimensional. Pushing acrylic stamps into the paint actually creates tactile texture (texture you can feel). It is a simple way to add dimension to your pages without adding bulk.

Supplies

Cardstock; textured cardstock (DCWV); patterned paper (My Mind's Eye); chipboard title (Miss Elizabeth's); acrylic stamps (Keller's Creations); alphabet stickers (American Crafts); sun and month stickers (Karen Foster Design); ribbon (Offray); Misc: acrylic paint, ink, scalloped circle punch, flower and tab punches

MATERIALS
ACRYLIC PAINT, FOAM BRUSH, CARDSTOCK, ACRYLIC STAMPS, PUNCHES

1 Use a foam brush to apply acrylic paint to cardstock. Paint an area that is slightly bigger than your acrylic stamp.

2 Press your acrylic stamp into the paint and let it dry.

3 Punch the desired shapes from the stamped area.

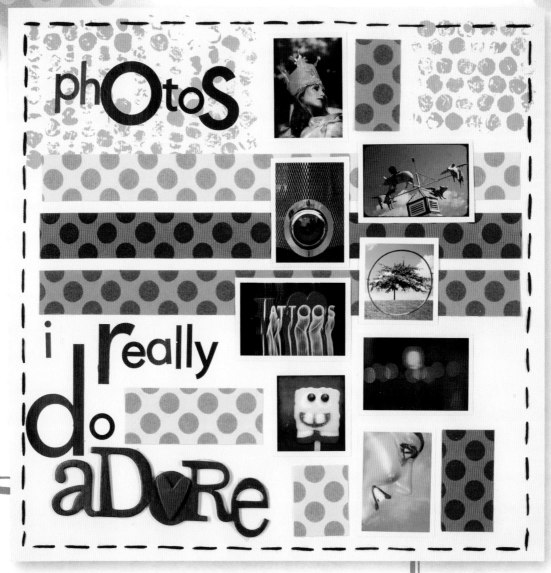

STAMP WITH BUBBLE WRAP AND ACRYLIC PAINT

Everyone has those photos that they absolutely love! Shannon combined some of hers into one fantastic layout even though the photos were of many different subjects. To add some texture to the layout, Shannon painted bubble wrap with acrylic paint and used it to stamp a pattern onto white cardstock. She tied the pattern and photos together with strips of bright paper in different colors in the same polka-dot pattern. The black stitching acts as a visual border that draws the eye to the photos.

Supplies

Patterned papers (The Paper Company); rub-ons (American Traditional Designs); chipboard title (Fancy Pants Designs); plastic heart (unknown); Misc: acrylic paint, bubble wrap

PAGE BY
SHANNON TAYLOR

30-45 MINUTES

STAMP WITH HOUSEHOLD ITEMS

Look around your house for interesting patterns and textures. Here are a few examples of stamping with items found around the house!

STAMP WITH A JAR GRIPPER AND GLITTER

One of the symptoms of an addiction to scrapbooking is looking everywhere for things to use on your scrapbook pages. On a trip to the dollar store, I saw this jar lid gripper and couldn't help but notice the interesting pattern. It made a great stamp. I love this technique of stamping with a glue pad and glitter. After stamping and glittering the image, I used a circle cutter to cut out the stamped image.

Supplies

Cardstock; patterned paper, felt accents, button, chipboard letters, scalloped border, ribbons, rub-ons (American Crafts); precut circle and scalloped circle (Keller's Creations); glitter (Martha Stewart Crafts); chipboard corners (Scenic Route); journaling tag (Making Memories); Misc: laser-cut paper, tickets, ink, glue

materials

JAR LID GRIPPER, GLUE INK PAD, PAPER, GLITTER, FOAM PLATE

30–45 MINUTES

1 Cover your jar gripper with glue ink by tapping the ink pad over the entire surface. Stamp the jar gripper on your background paper.

2 Immediately sprinkle the area with glitter.

3 Shake off excess glitter onto the plate and allow the glue to dry.

45-60
MINUTES

surrounding the cabin and nice flat ones down by the river. The kids washed the dirt off of the rocks, and painted

This cabin trip, I brought up craft paints, googly eyes, and the fabulous E-6000 glue. There are plenty of rocks

and glued all afternoon long. I think they would have kept going, but we ran out of paint and glue! I am always

Summer [2008]

YOU ROCK

amazed at the creativity of kids. We had lots of "pets," a cell-phone, a surfer on a surfboard, and multi-eyed aliens.

PAGE BY SHAUNTE WADLEY

STAMP WITH JARS AND ACRYLIC PAINT

Shaunte was so glad her kids were outside when she saw the mess they made painting these rocks! And once she saw the photos, she knew she wanted to incorporate paint into her layout, but keep it subtle because the photos were so busy. She painted the rims of jars from her kitchen—from spice jars to a peanut butter jar lid—to create the multicolored rings. Then she used a wooden spoon handle to stamp the white polka dots. Who needs expensive stamps when you have a cupboard full of lids?

Supplies

Cardstock; patterned paper (Pebbles); die cut alphabet and arrow border die (QuicKutz); brads (All Stuck Up, BoBunny); Misc: acrylic paint

ADD TEXTURE WITH TOY CAR TIRES AND ACRYLIC PAINT

Sixth grade is a difficult year. Some girls start to form cliques and are unkind to peers. Jen's daughter tries very hard to stay friends with everyone and be kind and patient with the girls, even when they are mean to her. Jen wanted her daughter to know how proud she is that she is tough and sticks to her guns. This cool technique was a great way to add a masculine touch to the pink color scheme. The toy truck tires added great texture and played off the rough and tough border at the bottom of the page.

Supplies

Cardstock; embossed cardstock (Doodlebug Design); patterned paper (Pebbles, BoBunny); chipboard elements (KI Memories, Making Memories, Heidi Swapp); tape border stickers (Heidi Swapp); twine (Craft Supply); buttons (American Crafts, Sonburn, BasicGrey); brads (Karen Foster Design); Misc: acrylic paint, photo corners; fonts: Century Gothic, Antique Type

Hardworking, smart, friendly, imaginative, and kind.

Lovely, diligent, talented, playful, creative, artistic, and all mine!

Compassionate, crazy, thoughtful, funny, and sweet!

She might just be a girl, but she knows just how to handle herself in a tough situation. I love to hear how she conquers bullies, includes everyone, and tries to make all her friends happy. I know it must be hard for her because sometimes it means that she is the one that gets left out of an activity. And sometimes those girls make fun of her (that makes me so mad to hear that), but she takes it in stride & keeps on smiling. Yep, I would have to say that she's definitely rough & tumble.

GIRL

UGHTOUGHROUGHTOUGHROUGH

60-90
MINUTES

PAGE BY JEN GALLACHER

41

mask a cool title

Masking is a fun and easy technique that is achieved by covering and then removing elements from your page to reveal the original background. Try these masking techniques for an interesting and textural page element.

MASK A COOL TITLE WITH MAGIC MESH AND ALPHABET STICKERS

I just adore mesh! I have found so many uses for it. This is one of my favorites. Adding texture and interest to your layouts is simple with this masking technique, and it is so easy to do. This technique can also be used directly on the page. You can mask anything you like or just use the pattern of the mesh as an accent.

Supplies

Cardstock; patterned paper (BasicGrey, My Mind's Eye, The Paper Studio); stickers (American Crafts); brads, felt accents (The Paper Studio); rub-ons (Sassafras Lass); ribbons (Crafts, Etc!, Target); circle cutter, pen (EK Success); mesh (Magic Mesh); label maker (DYMO); Misc: buttons, ink, acrylic paint, corner punch

45-60 MINUTES

materials

ALPHABET STICKERS, TAG, MESH, FOAM BRUSH, ACRYLIC PAINT, PAPER PLATE, PAPER TOWEL, TWEEZERS, MICRON PEN

1 Place your alphabet stickers on the tag.

2 Place the tag on a paper plate and cover the tag with adhesive mesh.

3 Dip the brush in paint and remove the excess on a paper towel. Paint over the mesh, feathering the edges to avoid a definite outline.

4 Remove the mesh. While the paint is wet, use tweezers to remove the stickers from the tag.

5 Once dry (about 10 minutes), trace the outline of the letters with a micron pen.

6 Place a second set of stickers offset from the outlined letters to create a shadow effect.

CRABS

One of Morgan's favorite things to do at the beach is to go crabbing. We head down to the swash and toss out our lines. Pulling in the line always seem to take forever while we wait with the net. We always catch a bucket full but let them all go before we head out. I dread the day when Morgan feels like she is too old to be out crabbing with her family.

Myrtle Beach, SC
June, 2007

Make It Frugal!

Try this technique with leftover stickers and use a different font for each letter for a whimsical title.

30-45 MINUTES

MASK A TITLE WITH STICKERS AND PENS

Crabbing is a tradition for our family when we visit the beach, so I'm never short on pictures of these trips. The title technique I used for this layout is so fast. You can use any stickers you like and any color pen! The crab stamp I found at a craft store was the perfect embellishment to add to this title.

Supplies

Cardstock; patterned paper (Making Memories); alphabet stickers (American Crafts); scalloped circle (The Paper Studio); ribbon brads (Karen Foster Design); brush pen (Marvy); stamp (Michaels); Misc: acrylic paint, ink, circle punches

Materials

LARGE AND SMALL ALPHABET STICKERS, BRUSH PEN, MICRON PEN, TWEEZERS

1 Place a large sticker letter of the first letter of the title on the page. Repeat with every other letter. Using a brush pen, brush over the letters, making sure the area immediately surrounding the stickers is covered well.

2 Use the micron pen to trace around the letters.

3 Remove the stickers with tweezers. Add the remaining letters with smaller alphabet stickers.

CUT IT OUT!

Circle cutters, punches and craft knives are great tools for creating openings in your layouts for embellishments, contrasting paper and decorative edges. These layouts will inspire some great cut out ideas.

CREATE A PATTERN WITH AN ANYWHERE HOLE PUNCH

Jen's husband is always doing sweet acts of service, and she wanted to document some of them. The funky patterned paper she chose for the page inspired a graphic pattern for the anywhere hole punch pattern. After punching the linear pattern with the hole punch, she mounted dark red cardstock behind two of the patterns and yellow behind the rest to set them off. This quick trick can be used to create any pattern anywhere on your page!

PAGE BY JEN GALLACHER

Supplies

Cardstock; patterned paper (BasicGrey, Scenic Route); buttons (American Crafts); scrapper's floss, rub-on letters (Karen Foster Design); paper lace borders (Doodlebug Design); letter stickers (Little Yellow Bicycle); Misc: photo corners, circle punches, anywhere hole punch; font: Uptown

30-45 MINUTES

CREATE A REVERSE SHAKER BOX

I was dying to use these little snowflake accents and thought a shaker box would be perfect, but I decided to add a little twist. The box goes behind the page this time! This reversed version has a totally different look than a traditional shaker box. One of the best things about all shaker boxes, reverse or otherwise, is that you can fill them full of anything you want. Beads, buttons, and snowflakes made the perfect accents for this snow page.

Supplies

Patterned paper (SEI, Cosmo Cricket); chipboard and sticker alphabets (American Crafts); stickers, journaling box, mesh ribbon (SEI); ribbon (Karen Foster Design); snowman accent, snowflake buttons (Wal-Mart); beads (Create-A-Craft); chipboard ring (Creek Bank Creations); foam tape (Therm O Web); Misc: ink, circle punch

PHOTOS BY
ALANA TURNER

60–90
MINUTES

materials

12" X 12" (30.5CM X 30.5CM) BACKGROUND PAPER, CIRCLE CUTTER, PLASTIC PACKAGING FILM, FOAM TAPE, BEADS, BUTTONS, SNOWFLAKES, SQUARE OF PAPER

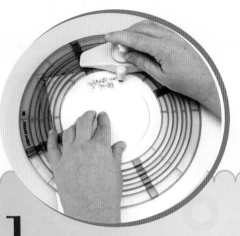

1
Cut a circle from the background paper with your circle cutter.

2
Add the plastic film from the product packaging to the page back, covering the circle.

3
On the back of the background paper, add the foam tape in a square around the cut-out circle, making sure the foam pieces meet at the four corners.

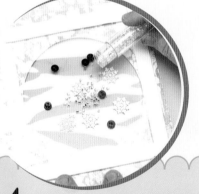

4
Add beads, buttons and other items to the square created by the foam tape.

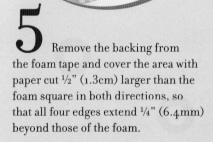

5
Remove the backing from the foam tape and cover the area with paper cut ½" (1.3cm) larger than the foam square in both directions, so that all four edges extend ¼" (6.4mm) beyond those of the foam.

Flips off the diving board, chasing underwater toys & eating yummy ice cream cake were just some of the fun activities that made Oliver's 9th birthday a huge success. John, Jami, Devan, Oliver, Robby & Dante had tons of fun at Haynesfied pool. Oliver loved that most of his gifts turned out to be cash. 2006

CUT SHAPES FROM PHOTOS

Shannon created a great pocket for her journaling by cutting a wave shape from her photo with a craft knife. She sanded around the shape to help it stand out and then cut similar shapes from various patterned papers and layered them on top of the photo. She printed her journaling on a circle and added a photo before tucking it into the wave cutout. Try this unique technique with any shape that fits your page theme.

Supplies

Patterned papers, lace ribbon, border, chipboard title (Chatterbox)

PAGE BY
SHANNON TAYLOR

60-90
MINUTES

CREATE A POSTAGE STAMP FRAME

Shannon created a postage stamp frame around her photos with a circle punch. After adhering the photos to white cardstock, she turned her circle punch upside down and punched half circles around the perimeter of the mat. She used postage stamp stickers under the plastic clock face to enhance the stamp theme on the page. What a creative theme for cruise photos!

Supplies

Patterned papers (My Mind's Eye, Prima); letter stickers (Doodlebug Design); plastic clock face (Hobby Lobby); Misc: foam adhesive, stamps; fonts: Courier, Claritty Bold

PAGE BY SHANNON TAYLOR

60-90 MINUTES

create a border

Borders don't have to be plain strips of paper. Check out these border ideas that can create texture, dimension or interest in your layouts.

30–45 MINUTES

DOODLE A BORDER WITH A DECORATIVE RULER AND PENS

Cruising was fantastic, and coming back to a clean cabin with a darling folded towel animal was so much fun. I wanted to create a layout for these photos that was light and playful. I love the casual look of hand-doodling but don't always like the way my hand doodling turns out. This quick and easy technique using a decorative ruler eliminates all those fears. Check out the swirl border on the journaling block; it's another doodling cheat done with a rub-on border.

Supplies

Cardstock; patterned paper (BasicGrey, Scenic Route); decorative ruler, alphabet and number stickers (Karen Foster Design); chipboard accents (Fancy Pants Designs); rub-ons (The Paper Studio); ribbons (American Crafts, Offray); micron pen (EK Success); white pen (Uni-ball)

MATERIALS

DECORATIVE RULER, BLACK MICRON PEN, WHITE GEL PEN

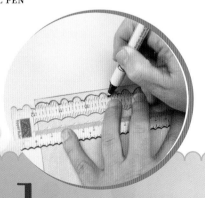

1 Using a micron pen, trace the edge of the decorative ruler.

2 Move the ruler a small amount and trace again.

3 Use a white gel pen to highlight the upper edges and add small circles.

The camera definitely loved Frankie from the very beginning. He was so adorable when he was a puppy. But as these photos show, I am not sure Frankie loved the camera as much as it loved him! That dangling strap was just too much for him to resist. As soon as he saw it swinging back and forth when I was trying to get a close shot of him he was all over it!

July 2005 ♥

love at first {sight}

FOLD A QUICK ACCORDION BORDER

The die cut borders on this page brought the layout together so quickly that I was able to take the time to create my own vertical border to separate the photos from the journaling. This accordion-folded border was easy and fun to make. It added texture and interest to the otherwise one-dimensional layout. Assembling the border before adhering it to the page made the construction easy because I could hold it in my hands while I worked. A die cut circle from the same sheet as the border takes the place of the "o" in the title, while the remaining letters were quickly stamped with foam stamps and chalk ink and then outlined with a pen.

Supplies

Cardstock; patterned paper (Wal-Mart); Scribble Scrabble die cuts (Scribble Scrabble); stickers (American Crafts); Misc: stamps, magnetic poetry, ink, staples

materials

12" (30.5CM) PAPER CUTTER, TWO COLORS OF THIN PAPER FOR 12" (30.5CM) STRIPS, RIBBON, ADHESIVE, STAPLER, STAPLES

1 Cut three ¾" (1.9cm) wide strips from two different colors of 12" (30.5cm) patterned paper (thin paper works best). Adhere the dark paper strips to the back of the light paper strips with ⅛" (3.2mm) of the dark paper showing.

2 Cut three 12" (30.5cm) strips of ¼" (6.4mm) wide ribbon and adhere them to the lighter paper. Pleat the first paper strip in 1" (2.5cm) folds, stapling each fold as you go.

3 Join the second and third strips by stapling, and continue pleating to extend the border to fit a 12" (30.5cm) page. Adhere to your page, folding any excess to the page back.

TRY a TITLE TecHNIQUE

Products for titles come in all shapes and sizes, but who says you have to use them as is? You can change any kind of product to get the color and look you want to achieve. These techniques can add color, texture and pizzazz to your titles.

materials

CHIPBOARD LETTERS, TISSUE PAPER, SCISSORS, FOAM BRUSH, DÉCOUPAGE MEDIUM, INK

60–90 MINUTES

CREATE CUSTOM LETTERS WITH TISSUE PAPER

Banana tissue paper—who knew?! After finding this adorable paper, I couldn't wait to use it on a scrapbook page. Using the paper to cover blank chipboard letters gave me the whimsical title I was looking for on this layout. Tissue paper comes in a huge number of colors and patterns, and the way it crinkles when you apply it adds interesting texture to flat letters.

Supplies

Cardstock; patterned paper (MMBI); scalloped circle, circle quote and precut ring (Keller's Creations; paper cut from Reminisce); tissue paper (American Greetings); large chipboard letter (DCWV); cursive chipboard letters (EK Success); alphabet stickers (American Crafts); tag (Li'l Davis Designs); chipboard circle (Creek Bank Creations); Misc: buttons, ink

1 Lay the chipboard letter on the tissue paper and cut a piece slightly larger than the letter. With a foam brush, paint a thin coat of découpage medium on the chipboard letter and place the paper on the front of the chipboard letter.

2 Add découpage medium to the back of the letter and fold the paper around the letter, clipping with scissors as needed.

3 Add a final coat of découpage medium to the letter. Ink the edges of the letter with a contrasting ink.

PHOTOS BY
NAN EVANS

CREATE CUSTOM CHIPBOARD LETTERS WITH A HOLE PUNCH

Chipboard letters are one of my favorite products for titles. I try to stretch my dollar as well as the versatility of the product by altering the letters to give them a different look for a variety of pages. For this layout, I covered the bare chipboard letters with coordinating die cuts and then used a hole punch to create a pattern that not only adds interest but also allows the color of the background paper to show through.

Supplies

Cardstock; patterned paper (BasicGrey); chipboard letters, die cuts (The Paper Loft); rub-ons (Fancy Pants Designs, American Crafts, Daisy D's); sticker letters (American Crafts); flowers (Prima); Misc: button, ink

15-30 MINUTES

DRESS UP A PRINTED TITLE WITH COLORED PENCILS

PAGE BY
SHANNON TAYLOR

I love this textured title that Shannon created with her printer and colored pencils. It emulates the texture in the corduroy dress this beautiful little girl has on. Shannon printed her title on cardstock and then placed it over a child's toy that had this great texture. Then she rubbed over the letters with a colored pencil and cut them out. This technique pulls out the pattern of the item, making the plain printed title more interesting and adding depth to the page. Look for interesting textures around your house to try this rubbing technique with.

45-60 MINUTES

Supplies

Patterned paper (K&Company, BasicGrey); colored pencils (EK Success); tree die cut (unknown); Misc: foam adhesive; fonts: Brody, Basic

girly

ashleigh is such a girly girl! she loves the glity and glam of all things femenine.

DRESS UP ALPHABET STICKERS WITH RUB-ONS

Girls are so much fun to dress up, and Ashleigh looks so adorable in all this pink! I knew these bright papers were the perfect match for these vibrant photos. I wanted the title and embellishments to contrast with the bright colors on the page, so I made those black and white. After adhering the white alphabet stickers, I outlined them with a black pen and used rub-ons directly on top to dress them up. The strong contrast between the black-and-white elements and the bright colors of the photos and background papers helps both to stand out as well as to complement each other.

Supplies

Cardstock; patterned paper, journaling block, metal clip, center ribbons (Making Memories); sticker alphabet, dotted ribbon (American Crafts); rub-ons (The Paper Studio); flower border (Doodlebug Design); flower (Prima); rhinestones (Darice); Misc: photo corners, micron pen, ink

30-45 MINUTES

PHOTOS BY ALANA TURNER

Make It Fabulous!

Place small accents of the same color around the page, like the black ones on this layout. It draws the eye around the page and makes the layout feel cohesive.

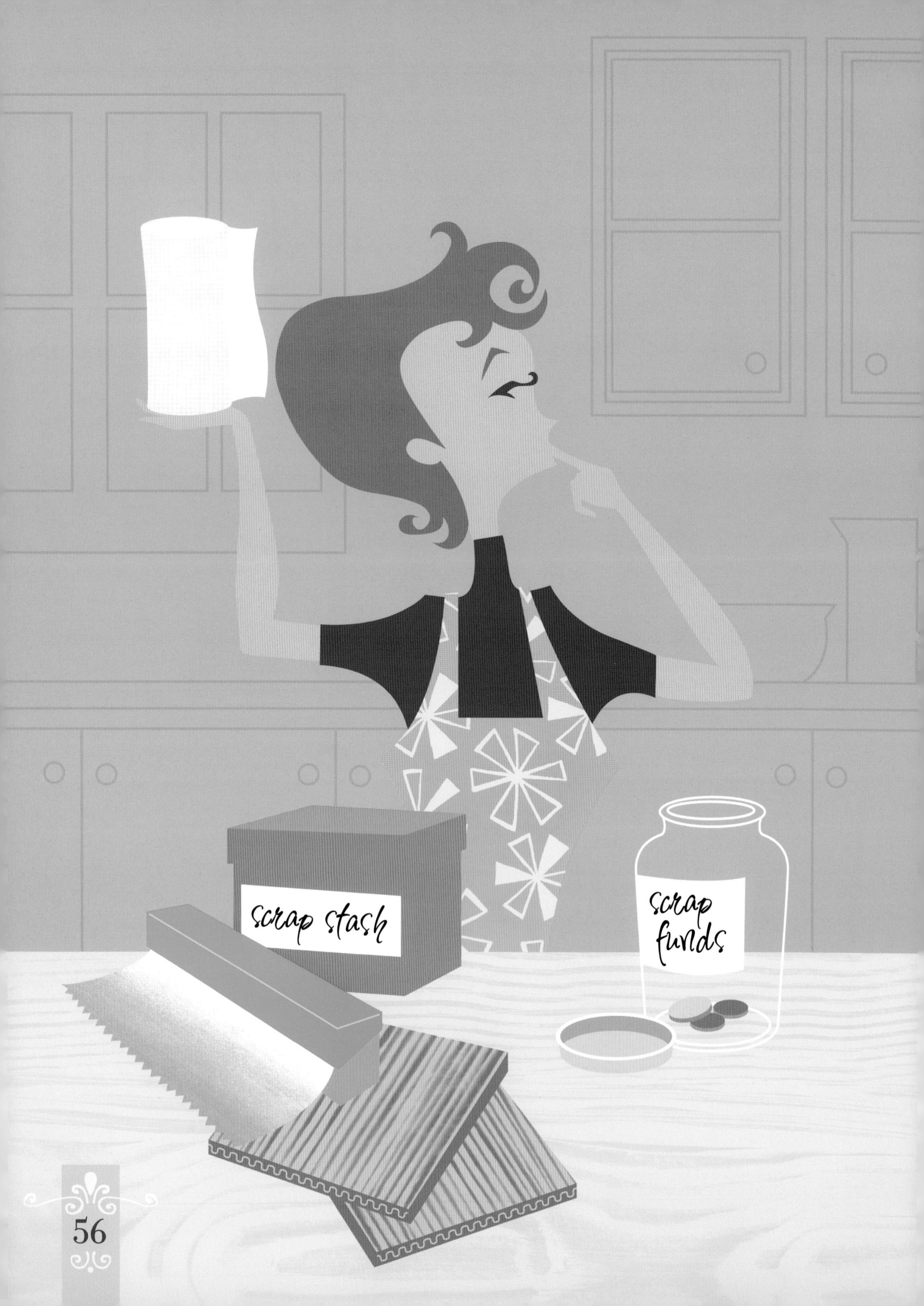
scrap stash
scrap funds

CHAPTER THREE

Frugal

With scrapbooking, there is always something you can spend your money on. There are the latest and greatest tools, the newest lines of paper and embellishments, and I always want them all! I am constantly looking for ways to stretch my scrapbooking dollar so I can buy the things I really want without feeling guilty.

This chapter is all about little tricks to save you some money. From using your scraps to seeing products you have in your stash in a new light, you will find tons of ideas and some new, cost-saving techniques to try as well. Read on to find great ways to squeeze some change out of your scrapbooking projects!

CUT UP YOUR PAPER SCRAPS

Everybody has those stacks of paper scraps they just can't bear to toss in the trash can. Pull them out and dust them off and try these techniques for some great page accents.

This journaling tag pulls out from behind one of the photos, allowing the space for four cropped photos along with the oversized egg.

CREATE AN OVERSIZED ELEMENT WITH SCRAPS

If you are like me, you have scraps of paper, ribbons and more that you just can't bear to part with. Make the most of that stack of leftovers by creating an oversized embellishment like this colorful egg. Draw your shape on a piece of white cardstock and trace it with a black pen so the shape can be seen through the back side of the paper. Turn the paper over and fill in the shape with strips of paper and ribbon. Cut out the shape and adhere it to the page. I edged this brightly colored egg with white paint to help it stand out from the background. Try this simple technique with any shape, theme or color scheme.

Supplies

Cardstock, scalloped circle (Bazzill Basics); patterned paper (Karen Foster Design); paper scraps for egg (The Paper Studio, DCWV, BoBunny); chipboard elements (Heidi Swapp); tag (Keller's Creations); ribbon (American Crafts, Offray); ric rack (Offray); rub-ons (Sassafras Lass); white pen (Uni-ball); Misc: paint, buttons

the land of cotton

West Tennessee if full of cotton fields, and when we saw this one that hadn't been picked we decided to stop and use it as a history lesson for the kids. As they picked a couple of pieces and pricked their fingers we reminded them of the slaves that had to pick those fields by hand in the hot sun for no money. Those cotton fields will always be a reminder of that sad time in our state's history.

08

45-60 MINUTES

PAPER PIECE YOUR ACCENTS FROM SCRAPS

This cotton field was truly an amazing sight, and I couldn't wait to scrapbook these photos. To keep the cost down on this layout, I paper pieced my own cotton accents out of my scraps. Looking at the plants in the photos, I drew the cotton on white paper and cut out each piece with sharp scissors. I traced the paper cotton onto dark brown paper and then drew the stalk and pod around the traced image so the two pieces would fit together correctly on the layout. After inking the edges of the pieces for definition, I put the cotton embellishments together on the page for the perfect accent to my pictures.

Supplies

Patterned paper (The Paper Loft, Cosmo Cricket, BasicGrey); chipboard letters and numbers (American Crafts); sticker letters (American Crafts, Making Memories); chipboard circle (Creek Bank Creations); trim (Fancy Pants Designs); circle cutter (EK Success); Misc: corner punch, ink

PUNCH FROM YOUR SCRAPS

Take out your punches and those scraps of paper and create fantastic accents, backgrounds and borders for your pages for free.

PAGE BY
JEN GALLACHER

60–90 MINUTES

PUNCH CARDSTOCK COVERED WITH MESH

Jen wanted her layout to have the same bright, creative and colorful feel that her daughter's artwork possesses. She chose a vibrant green to create this fun mesh accent. She punched circles from both the mesh and a coordinating piece of cardstock and then layered the mesh on top. Jen thought the mesh circles, felt buttons and cute metal tags reflected her daughter's fun personality. Check out the little bit of mesh Jen placed in the A's in her title. So cute!

Supplies

Cardstock; patterned paper, leather alphabet letters, chipboard letters and brackets, buttons (American Crafts); mesh (Magic Mesh); felt buttons, metal tags, chipboard heart (Making Memories); safety pins (Making Memories, Déjà Views); embossing folder, die cutting machine (Cuttlebug for Provo Craft); scrapper's floss (Karen Foster Design); Misc: corner rounder, office punch, circle punches; font: Hattenschweiler

Now that you're almost 9, we don't go to parks much

Hang

cLimb

SPiN

middle of it. Let's just say... you had a

anymore. But we found one by accident recently that had a merry-go-round. I was
so excited to take your picture while standing in the

PUNCH A PATTERNED BACKGROUND

Boys never slow down, as these photos of Shannon's son will attest.
She was able to create a fantastic sense of movement with this punched
background. To save money on this page, Shannon rummaged through
her paper scraps and picked random pieces with lots of color. After
punching her scraps with a circle punch, she adhered them to the page,
alternating between flat and raised adhesives. This is an inexpensive
way to create a patterned background. The raised adhesives give the
page lots of dimension, and alternating the adhesives gives the page
a sense of movement.

PAGE BY
SHANNON TAYLOR

60–90
MINUTES

Supplies

Patterned paper (Artistic Scrapper, BoBunny, Dream Street Papers, Scenic Route, SEI and
other scraps); alphabet stickers (K&Company); brads (BoBunny); Misc: pen, foam adhesive

MIKAYLA

Age Five

cativ

play

lo

I am a lucky mommy; not only to know you, and love you, but to call you my own.

PAGE BY
SHAUNTE WADLEY

PUNCH A BORDER FROM SCRAPS

Shaunte is always excited to use up her ever-growing scrap stash! This punched border is a perfect way for her to save money by taking advantage of the scraps and to add subtle color to her layout. She used a large circle punch, sliced the circles in half, and adhered them to the page. Once the circles were in place, Shaunte added the journaling strip to hide the seams. Such a quick and adorable layout!

Supplies

Cardstock (Core'dinations); patterned paper (BoBunny, Doodlebug Design, K&Company, 7gypsies, Scenic Route); foam alphabet (American Crafts); shamrock buttons (Provo Craft)

30-45 MINUTES

SK8R

Jayden {2008}

Xtreme

60–90 MINUTES

PAGE BY
SHAUNTE WADLEY

PUNCH AND USE BOTH POSITIVE AND NEGATIVE SPACE

Shaunte loves using stars on the layouts she does of her boys. This time she saved some money by punching the stars out of her tags and then using the punched images as embellishments on her page. With the bottom of the tags tucked under the photos, no one will see where the extra stars were punched. Stretch your scrapbooking dollar by using both the positive and negative spaces from your punches.

Supplies

Cardstock; patterned paper (BoBunny); die cut border and alphabet (QuicKutz); eyelets (Karen Foster Design); Misc: ink, star punch

recycle, reuse, repurpose

In your kitchen drawers and in the trash in your scrapbook room are all kinds of things you can reuse or repurpose. Check out these recycling techniques that can save you cash as well as create some fantastic scrapbook pages.

PHOTOS BY DEB CARDIN

45–60 MINUTES

CREATE A TITLE WITH A PENCIL ERASER AND PAINT

Finding titles that work with your layout can be challenging, so why not paint your own? This technique couldn't be easier, and it can be done in any space and shape because you pencil the letters in yourself. The best part is that this fantastic, custom look can be achieved with things you have lying around the house for virtually no cost!

Supplies

Cardstock; patterned paper (Fancy Pants Designs); chipboard swirls (The Paper Studio); chipboard frame and bird (American Crafts); scalloped circle (Keller's Creations); white pen (Uni-ball); micron pen (EK Success); Misc: acrylic paint, ink

MATERIALS
NEW PENCIL, ACRYLIC PAINT, MICRON PEN

1 Write your title in pencil, spacing each letter to accommodate paint dots.

2 Using a new pencil eraser, dip the eraser lightly in acrylic paint and stamp along the pencil lines. Retouch the paint after each print and wipe the eraser clean every 2–3 dots.

3 After the paint dries, add circles and highlights with a micron pen.

♥ Pure 005423

happiness

It started innocently enough. I promised to keep Robby in our bed at night only while nursing, but **11** years later he's still in our bed. So when Oliver was born I promised he'd sleep in a crib. He did for **10** months until I got scared when he began climbing out over the hardwood floor. Can you guess where he still sleeps? They aren't scared to sleep alone, it's just for the comfort of our close knit family. Rob & I actually love it. We realize that this will end so very soon so we cherish every evening. And the boys absolutely love it!

PAGE BY
SHANNON TAYLOR

45-60
MINUTES

(EXCLUDING
DRYING TIME)

CREATE A CUSTOM BACKGROUND WITH RUBBER BANDS AND DIMENSIONAL GLOSS MEDIUM

What an amazing and economical technique Shannon used to create her background paper! She placed 6 to 8 rubber bands on various patterned papers and filled them in with Diamond Glaze. After letting them dry overnight, Shannon cut them out and added them to a cardstock background. She filled in the remainder of the cardstock with rubber bands and repeated the Diamond Glaze treatment. Once the background was dry, she added her photos, title and journaling. Shannon put the pieces aside while they dried and worked on other layouts. The drying time of this treatment may take a while, but it is so worth it for this cool look!

Supplies

Patterned papers (BoBunny, Daisy Bucket Designs, Pink Paislee); happiness die cut (My Mind's Eye); ticket (Jenni Bowlin); alphabet stamps (Hero Arts); Diamond Glaze (JudiKins); Misc: foam adhesive, rubber bands; font: Balker

45–60
MINUTES

USE A FRAME CUT
FROM A LARGE CIRCLE

Of all the tools I own, my circle cutter is without a doubt my favorite. I love having the ability to cut circles of all different sizes. To create the frame on this page, center the circle cutter on the page before cutting, remove the cut circle and then place the frame over a contrasting piece of patterned paper. It looks great, and the circle that was cut out can be used on another page, giving you more bang for your buck with your scrapbooking paper.

Supplies

Cardstock; patterned paper (Scenic Route); chipboard letters, circle cutter (EK Success); chipboard mushrooms and flowers (Sassafras Lass); alphabet and number stickers (American Crafts); tags (Avery); Misc: acrylic paint, ink

PHOTOS BY PAUL KETRON

On a train from London to Haywards Heath a chance meeting with a local man and his son returning from a soccer game led us to a beautiful town about thirty minutes south of where we were staying. He told us of his hometown of Lewes with its beautiful scenery and majestic castle and we decided to make the journey and see it for ourselves. This quaint little town he spoke of was well worth the trip.

15-30 MINUTES

PHOTOS BY
PAUL KETRON

USE A LARGE CIRCLE CUT FROM A FRAME

Always one to make the most of what I have, I created this layout with the circle that I cut from the paper on the facing page. Rather than just place the large circle on the page as an accent, I cut it in half and put the straight edges toward the outside of the background paper. This placement of the circle halves adds curves to the page that coordinate with the swirls in the title and provides contrast to the straight line of the photos.

Supplies

Cardstock; patterned paper (Scenic Route, The Paper Loft); chipboard elements (Fancy Pants Designs); chipboard letters (Heidi Swapp); chipboard buckle (Colorbök); stamp (Stampabilities); journaling tag (Making Memories); ribbon (Offray); Misc: ink

STAMP A JOURNALING AREA WITH CORRUGATED CARDBOARD

I am always looking for new ways to add journaling to my pages. This cardboard circle was part of the packaging in some dinnerware at a discount store, so I asked the clerk if I could have it. I loved the circular shape of the cardboard, and when I saw the corrugated lines on the back, I knew it would be the perfect stamp for journaling. It not only made a perfect place to tell the story of the day, but it also added an interesting and textural element to the layout.

Supplies

Patterned paper (Fancy Pants Designs, American Crafts); alphabet stickers (American Crafts, EK Success); ribbon (Offray, BasicGrey); Misc: buttons, acrylic paint, ink, cardboard circle, tab punch

materials

CORRUGATED CARDBOARD, ACRYLIC PAINT, FOAM BRUSH, MICRON PEN

1 Use a foam brush to coat the cardboard with acrylic paint (work quickly with thick coverage).

2 Stamp the cardboard onto the background paper, pressing in all areas.

3 After the paint dries (10–15 minutes), journal with a micron pen.

3rd Grade

mrs. hammonds

Isaac absolutely adores Mrs. Hammonds. The first day of school he came home saying "Mom, she is so funny!" Every day he jumps up and is excited to go to school and learn and I know that the biggest influence of his attitude about school is her. We feel very blessed [to have a] teacher who loves him. [That] gives him the [best 3rd] grade experience!

30–45 MINUTES

REUSE A CARDBOARD STAMP

Recognize the cardboard circle on this page? That's right! It is the corrugated circle I used to stamp a journaling area on the "Summertime" layout on the facing page. After stamping with the circle, I left it to dry so I could throw it in the garbage, but I changed my mind when I saw how cool it looked. It makes the perfect accent for this school page and, just like the image it stamped, it adds fabulous texture. I got accents for two pages for the price of one, which was no cost at all!

Supplies

Cardstock; patterned paper, border sticker (Scenic Route); chipboard alphabet (Heidi Swapp); chipboard ring (Creek Bank Creations); school stickers (Karen Foster Design); rub-ons (The Paper Studio); Misc: acrylic paint, binder clip, ink, cardboard circle

PHOTOS BY NAN EVANS

Moving to Little Rock from Birmingham wasn't easy. Brandon was starting college at Tuscaloosa and it would be our third move in six years. We were closer to family but farther from friends and once again...we were starting over. Finding this house was a long process, but making it feel like home will take time and lots of love.

60-90 MINUTES

MAKE YOUR OWN CHIPBOARD BUTTONS

Like the look of chipboard buttons? Making your own is a simple process, and you can match them to the paper on your layout. Try using shapes other than a traditional round button. This layout features buttons that are rounded squares and scalloped circles.

Supplies

Cardstock; patterned paper (Scenic Route, My Mind's Eye); chipboard alphabet (Heidi Swapp); chipboard bracket (The Paper Studio); alphabet stickers (Making Memories); Crystal Lacquer, ribbon (Michaels, Fancy Pants Designs, Offray); Misc: ink, circle punch, scalloped punches, tag punch, corner punch

materials

CHIPBOARD, PUNCHES, PATTERNED PAPER, ADHESIVE, HOLE PUNCH, CRYSTAL LACQUER, RIBBON

1 Punch the chipboard into circles and squares of different sizes. Punch the patterned paper with the same punches and adhere the pieces to the chipboard.

2 Use a hole punch to make holes in the centers of the punchouts. Ink the edges.

3 Cover the pieces with Crystal Lacquer. Add ribbon if desired.

inexpensive typography ideas

Title and journaling products can add up, and cutting the cost can be a challenge. These inexpensive typography ideas are fun and won't break the bank.

HANDWRITE YOUR TITLE

Pens are such an economical supply to have on hand. For less than three dollars, you can have a good quality pen that can be used for so many different things, including your titles. Many people are afraid to write on their pages, and I used to be one of them. Now I find that if I write my title lightly in pencil first, I can correct anything I don't like before I commit to the pen. After tracing over the pencil lines with a black pen, I simply add a few highlights with a white gel pen and love the results!

Supplies

Cardstock; patterned paper (BoBunny); stamp (Studio G); alphabet stickers (American Crafts); ric rack, printed ribbon, brads (Karen Foster Design); fabric brad (The Paper Studio); label maker (DYMO); Misc: colored pencils, micron pen, white pen, buttons, ink

ALTER A COMPUTER-GENERATED TITLE WITH ACRYLIC PAINT

PHOTOS BY BARBARA KETRON

The pictures my mother took of sea turtles on the beach in Hawaii were so amazing that I really wanted to make a special layout for her to remember the experience. I love to use this painting technique when I want to make a standout title. It has the look of a completely hand-painted element and the ease of beginning with a computer-generated title. I chose the chipboard accent because it is reminiscent of seaweed and made the perfect embellishment for this layout.

Supplies

Cardstock; patterned paper (Cosmo Cricket, My Mind's Eye, Jenni Bowlin); chipboard elements (Fancy Pants Designs); rub-ons (The Paper Studio); alphabet stickers (Wordsworth); ribbon, number stickers (Piggy Tales); Misc: acrylic paint, ink, micron pen, binder clip, corner and tag punches

60–90 MINUTES

materials

PRINTED TITLE, ACRYLIC PAINT, PAINTBRUSH,
MICRON PEN

1 Using a wet brush and a small amount of acrylic paint a shade darker than the ink, brush on one edge of each letter to create a shadow effect.

2 Using a thin brush and white paint, make highlights opposite the shaded areas.

3 Outline the title with a black micron pen.

USE CARDSTOCK IN A LABEL MAKER

I love the look of journaling done with a label maker, but if you use the tape that comes with the label maker, you are limited to the tape colors the company produces. You can have endless color possibilities by running cardstock through instead! (Make sure your cardstock has a white core or use paper with a white back.) Just cut strips of paper the width of the label tape and thread it through the label maker. Gently sand over the raised letters with an emery board or fine sandpaper, being careful to expose just the white core or back of the paper. On this layout I added white paint to the edges of the strips and some staples to the ends.

Supplies

Cardstock; patterned paper (My Mind's Eye, Sassafras Lass); tags, rub-ons, sticker letters, staples (Making Memories); blue sticker letter (Sonburn); stamps (Magnetic Poetry); label maker (DYMO); lobster stickers (Creative Memories); ribbon (Offray); dimensional glaze (Aleene's); Misc: ink, tab punch

Make It Fast!

Scrapbooking is like cooking; if you pace it right, it all comes together at the same time. Begin by doing any steps that require drying, like painting, stamping or glazing, and set those pieces aside while you work on the rest of the layout. I made the lobster tag with dimensional glaze first on this layout to give it time to dry and stamped the title last before I set the page aside to dry.

PHOTOS BY ALANA TURNER

ACCENT CHIPBOARD WITH LEFTOVER RUB-ONS

If you are like me, you have partial sheets of rub-ons left over from numerous projects. This rub-on remnant was actually an "oops." Part of the rub-on got stuck to my work surface when I started to use it on another project, leaving only a partial image. I thought about trashing it, but when I saw the large chipboard letter, I knew it would be a great place to take advantage of my mistake. Waste not, want not!

Supplies

Cardstock; patterned paper (Daisy D's, Fancy Pants Designs, My Mind's Eye); chipboard letter (DCWV); die cuts (Daisy D's); rub-ons (BasicGrey); ribbon (Making Memories); ric rack (Fancy Pants Designs); brad (Karen Foster Design); Misc: buttons, acrylic paint, ink, circle punches

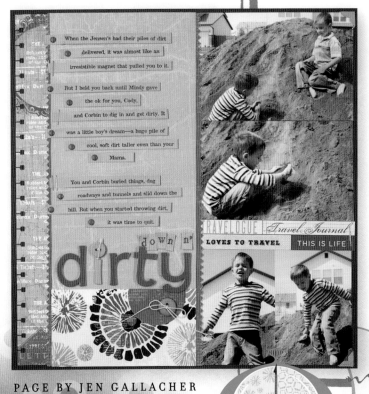

PAGE BY JEN GALLACHER

JOURNAL ON PAINTED STRIPS

A pile of dirt…what boy could ask for more? Jen used a great trick to create a dirty look for her journaling. Using a foam brush, she put a rough coat of acrylic paint on a piece of cardstock. After the paint dried she ran the cardstock through the computer and printed her journaling. After she cut the journaling into strips, she used staples and brads to attach them to the layout for a great look with her dirty photos.

Supplies

Cardstock; patterned paper (Little Yellow Bicycle); brads (Karen Foster Design); chipboard letters (Scenic Route); buttons (American Crafts, Jo-Ann); letter stamps (PSX Design); twine (Craft Supply); Misc: spiral notebook punch, circle punch, staples, pinking scissors, photo corners, acrylic paint; font: Antique Type

Make It Fabulous!

This is a travel-themed line of patterned paper and embellishments, but the grungy look and rich colors matched Jen's dirt pictures perfectly. Look outside the box when it comes to themed papers.

EASY SLIDE MOUNT ACCENTS

Remember those slide mounts you have in your drawer? They can make some adorable accents for your pages, so pull them out and try these page ideas to make the most of a product you may have forgotten about.

Fall in Tennessee is always so beautiful. I love to see the leaves change to brilliant reds and warm golds A trip to Fall Creek Falls didn't disappoint when I saw these striking leaves on the trees in the campground and snapped these pictures. They are a constant reminder of nature's beauty.

30-45 MINUTES

CREATE MARBLED PHOTO CORNERS

Finding new uses for products is a great way to stretch your scrapbooking dollar. These photo corners are made from one cardstock slide mount marbled with chalk ink. The round opening in the center of the slide mount creates an interesting detail when it is cut in half. The circular shape mimics the chipboard dots in the title and the paper circles in the background. The bright colors of the leaves in the photos pop against the earthy tones in the papers and embellishments, while the slide mount photo corners create a visual outline that highlights the striking photos.

Supplies

Cardstock; patterned paper (The Paper Studio); slide mount, chipboard circles (Keller's Creations); alphabet stickers (American Crafts, Wal-Mart); chipboard ring (Gin-X); chipboard bracket (The Paper Studio); mesh (Magic Mesh); chalk ink (Clearsnap)

Make It Fabulous!

Repeating shapes within a layout creates continuity and helps direct the eye around the page. In this layout, the small chipboard circles create a visual triangle with the title, month and year.

MATERIALS

CARDSTOCK SLIDE MOUNT, CHALK INK, SCISSORS, DARK INK

1 Tear a cardstock slide mount in half to make two squares.

2 With chalk ink and using a swirling motion, tint the slide mount until it reaches the desired shade. (The swirling creates the marbled effect.)

3 Cut each square in half, creating four photo corners. Ink the edges of the photo corners with a darker ink to finish.

FRAME PHOTOS WITH SLIDE MOUNTS

The backgrounds on these rainforest photos were so similar that they seemed to get lost when I put them next to each other on the layout. I have stacks of slide mounts in my stash, and using them as photo frames gives definition to each photo and keeps me from having to mat them. The simple color-blocked background was so quick to put together, and repeating the square shape in the photos and background gives the layout continuity.

Supplies

Cardstock; patterned paper (BasicGrey, MMBI); slide mounts (Keller's Creations); chipboard accent (BasicGrey); alphabet stickers (The Paper Loft, American Crafts, Making Memories); ribbon (Offray); Misc: ink

PHOTOS BY MORGAN FESMIRE

CREATE A BOW BORDER WITH SLIDE MOUNTS

I am not used to scrapbooking myself! After fourteen years of being overweight and hiding from the camera, even eighty-seven pounds lighter I still have a hard time having my picture taken. I'm not a very girly girl, but I did want this layout of me to be somewhat feminine. This bow border idea came quite by accident. I had two slide mounts lying on my table—one open, one closed—and I noticed that it looked like a bow! I ran a strip of paper through the slide mounts to create the look of a bow buckle and voila! It is quick and easy and gave me the feminine look I wanted without being too girly.

Supplies

Patterned paper (cherryArte, Scenic Route, Jenni Bowlin); rub-ons (cherryArte); slide mounts (Keller's Creations); flowers, alphabet stickers (American Crafts); chipboard corners (Scenic Route); rhinestone brads (Karen Foster Design); ribbon (Michaels, Karen Foster Design, Wrights); Misc: paper clip, ink

RIBBON accents

Ribbon is inexpensive, so it makes a fantastic, cost-effective accent for scrapbook pages. You can use even the smallest bit of ribbon on your pages, so find a place to store your little pieces. Try these ideas to make the most of every inch of ribbon.

Little Miss Sunshine

Lily Belle has that inner sparkle that her mother had as a child. It's that extra something that makes total strangers stop & stare. Her whole face lights up & you can't help smiling with her. She really just glows.

2008

45-60 MINUTES

CREATE QUICK TWISTED-RIBBON-AND-WIRE ACCENTS OR TITLES

PAGE BY
SHANNON TAYLOR

I don't know about you, but I have enough ribbon to cover the walls of my scrapbook room! I am constantly looking for new ways to incorporate it into my pages, and this twisted technique of Shannon's is so cool I can't wait to try it myself. She cut ribbon and heavy wire the same length and folded them in half. To keep the wire and ribbon even, she poked one end of the wire through the middle of the ribbon and then twisted them together until the wire was completely covered. Then she bent the ends back to keep them from poking the layout and tied a knot in the end of the ribbon. You can bend this covered wire into shapes, words or anything you want!

Supplies

Patterned papers, title piece, rub-on (October Afternoon); wire (Artistic Wire); ribbon (Wal-Mart); fibers (Making Memories, Fibers by the Yard); Misc: font: Marketing Script

PAGE BY JEN GALLACHER

60–90 MINUTES

USE YOUR CAST-OFF RIBBON SCRAPS

Jen watched her children try to fly their kite to no avail. She knew that they needed more wind and a good tail for their kite. As she started her layout, she thought about the kite tail and pulled out her ribbon scraps to create her own. She added more ribbon scraps as a border, taking advantage of remnants that might otherwise be gathered up and thrown in the garbage can. The result is this gorgeous layout with ribbon accents that make perfect pops of color!

Supplies

Cardstock; patterned paper (KI Memories, Chatterbox, Scenic Route, Fancy Pants Designs); brads (Karen Foster Design); chipboard and leather alphabets, buttons (American Crafts); ribbon (Offray, Karen Foster Design, American Crafts); twine (Craft Supply); Misc: photo corners, circle punch, scalloped scissors; font: 2Peas Roxie

Make It Frugal!

Have a specific place to keep your ribbon scraps, no matter how small. I have a small drawer in a desktop container where I keep mine, and I add them to pages as accents all the time.

PAGE BY JEN GALLACHER

30–45 MINUTES

MAKE PHOTO CORNERS WITH RIBBON SCRAPS

With a five-year-old boy, Jen never knows what kind of photos she's going to get—a happy smile or a cheesy grin like the one in the photo in the center of this layout. She couldn't wait to scrap these photos and turned to her stash of leftover ribbon for some great accents. Jen mitered the corners on these small pieces of ribbon and made them into oversized photo corners. She folded another small piece of ribbon and stapled it under her photo mat for another quick, cost-conscious embellishment.

Supplies

Cardstock; alphabet stickers, felt heart, tags (American Crafts); buttons (American Crafts, Jo-Ann); scrapper's floss (Karen Foster Design); Misc: photo corners, scalloped scissors, circle punches; font: Century Gothic

keep it simple

Sometimes one of the easiest ways to save money is to just keep things simple. These pages are streamlined, cost-effective and come together very quickly.

LET THE PATTERNED PAPER WORK FOR YOU

Don't blink because when you do, those sweet little babies become teenagers before you know it. My daughter is fourteen now, and I wanted to capture how she is getting older and becoming a beautiful young woman right before my eyes. This patterned paper provides a beautiful background that requires nothing more than a title and a simple tag embellishment. The paper's black ring provided the perfect spot for the date, while the preprinted lines on the paper made quick work of the journaling.

Supplies

Cardstock; patterned paper (BasicGrey); alphabet stickers (American Crafts, Karen Foster Design); number stickers (Karen Foster Design); rub-ons (The Paper Studio); ribbon (American Crafts)

15-30 MINUTES

The pumpkin patch raised money for missions and we had such a great time lining up and passing the pumpkins down a line of volunteers to separate into the piles of fall colors.

Saint Mark's UMC
Birmingham, AL

October, 2006

15-30
MINUTES

USE MULTIPLE PHOTOS

These photos are absolutely gorgeous, and I just couldn't bring myself to crop them or leave any of them off the layout. Once I had the photos placed on the page, it took very few products to create the title and journaling areas. I double-layered the chipboard letters to create a shadow effect on the photo. This layout is one of my favorites!

Supplies

Cardstock; patterned paper (Fancy Pants Designs, Bazzill Basics); chipboard alphabet (American Crafts); ribbon (Piggy Tales); brad (Karen Foster Design); flower (Bazzill Basics); button (Junkits); Misc: ink, scalloped punch

Make It Fabulous!

Save some space on your page by placing your title directly on a photo, but make sure you don't cover anything of importance.

scrap WITH HOUSEHOLD ITEMS

From stamping to painting, you can find ways to use items you find around your home. Think outside the box and look for ways to incorporate inexpensive items into your techniques or directly on your pages.

boy, n: a noise with dirt on it.

Wishing that we had our own patch of grass so that I could watch you do this every day—play in the water. Corbin and Cody invited you over for a splash on their slip n' slide. You had no idea how to "slip", but you thoroughly enjoyed cooling off on a hot summer day. I'm really looking forward to a time when I can sit on our own deck or patio and watch you and Katelyn make some waves of your own. I'm sure you'll be pretty happy about that yourselves! (July 17, 2008)

PAGE BY JEN
GALLACHER

45-60 MINUTES

PUNCH FROM PLAYING CARDS

Jen simply punched circles from playing cards to use as bubble accents on the layout. The color and pattern were perfect for this all-boy page. Using pop dots under a few of the circles added some dimension to the bubbles. She also cut the corner from an extra playing card to create a large photo corner for the layout. This technique provided a quick and completely free accent because the cards were leftovers from a deck.

Supplies

Cardstock; patterned paper (Pebbles, Chatterbox); boy die cut (Pebbles); bead chain (Wal-Mart); playing cards (Streamline); pop dots (All Night Media); brads (Karen Foster Design); Misc: photo corners, font: Hattenschweiler

Make It Frugal!

You can run playing cards through die cut machines, use them with punches, hand cut them, use them as paper piece, etc. The ideas are endless!

tropical

HOT CHOCOLATE

For days, Oliver begged his grandma Becky for mini umbrellas. What a strange request for an 8 year old kid! Once he got his wish, he wanted hot chocolate with a curly straw & an umbrella stabbed into a marshmellow. I've never heard of a tropical hot chocolate drink before, but he sure was satisfied! Weird!

SCRAP WITH KITCHEN ITEMS

PAGE BY SHANNON TAYLOR

Shannon's layout is so fun and colorful! This unique topic required some unique embellishments. She found a cheap bamboo placemat and cut a long strip to use as an accent. Because her son was using the umbrella in his hot chocolate, she added a few to the page to add color and whimsy and to support the tropical title. This idea is just as cute as her son is!

Supplies

Patterned paper (BasicGrey); paper umbrellas (unknown); bamboo placemat (Target); clear grid overlay (Pageframe Designs); foam alphabet stickers (American Crafts); glitter brads (Creative Imaginations); Misc: fonts: Hawaiian Punk, Gilligan's Island

30-45 MINUTES

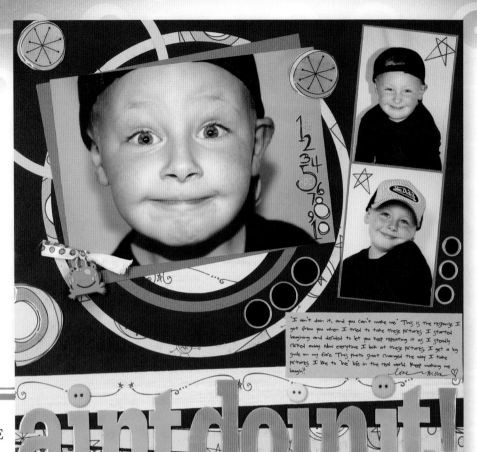

PAGE BY JULIE JOHNSON

45–60
MINUTES

CREATE A UNIQUE EMBELLISHMENT WITH WASHERS

Who wouldn't love a face like this? Julie had so much fun with this colorful layout. Her washer technique is so cute and didn't cost her a dime! She added the dimensional glaze to her title to tie it in with the embellishments. Check out your garage cabinets and your toolbox for interesting objects that you can incorporate into your scrapbook pages.

Supplies

Cardstock; patterned paper, ribbon (Autumn Leaves); cardstock letters (Gin-X); dimensional glaze (Aleene's); frog (Around The Block); metal glue (Making Memories); Misc: scissors, washers

MATERIALS

WASHERS, GLUE FOR METAL, BACKGROUND PAPER, DIMENSIONAL GLAZE, SCISSORS

1 Glue a washer to the background paper with adhesive suitable for metals.

2 Add dimensional glaze to the center of the washer and allow it to dry. Cut out the washer embellishments with sharp scissors.

i find you very dreamy!

There are moments in life when a mother glances across a room at her beautiful child as if she's seeing him for the first time. Then an instant later she remembers that this gorgeous boy belongs to her. She can't believe her luck that she is his mom and he looks at her with such love. He truly is dreamy. -Robby 2008

60-90 MINUTES

SCRAPBOOK WITH COTTON BALLS

Shannon wanted to create the dreamy look of clouds on her layout. She used cotton balls she found in the cabinet to create the cloud effect and then used white embroidery thread to adhere the cotton balls to the layout with a large cross stitch over each one. You never know what you might find in your closet to create a "dreamy" page like this one.

Supplies

Patterned paper (K&Company, Scenic Route); letter stickers (American Crafts); buttons (Foof-A-La); embroidery floss (DMC); Misc: cotton balls, font: Klemscott Roman

PAGE BY SHANNON TAYLOR

Make It Fast!

Don't have time to stitch the cotton balls on? Use an acid-free tacky glue to adhere them. Be sure to allow the glue to dry completely before putting your page in a protector.

PAGE BY JEN GALLACHER

EMBOSS ALUMINUM FOIL

What could be more cost-effective than searching your drawers for kitchen items to scrap with? I absolutely love this aluminum foil technique that Jen used on this adorable robot page. The texture and pattern created with the embossing is amazing, and the shine of the aluminum foil is the perfect touch on this retro-inspired page. Check out the border strip across the bottom. Jen covered cardstock in aluminum foil and crimped one end.

Supplies

Cardstock; patterned paper (KI Memories, Sandylion); chipboard letter stickers (American Crafts); embossing folder and machine (Cuttlebug for Provo Craft); crimper (Gill Mechanical Company); chipboard star and brackets (Maya Road); robot charm (Karen Foster Design); Misc: corner punch, circle punch; font: Blue Plate Special

Materials

CARDSTOCK, ALUMINUM FOIL, CIRCLE CUTTER OR PUNCH, EMBOSSING PLATE, EMBOSSING MACHINE

1 Adhere the aluminum foil to the cardstock. Cut a circle with a circle cutter.*

If using a punch for smaller circles, run the cardstock covered in aluminum foil through the machine first and then punch.

2 Place the circle in the embossing plate and run the plate through the embossing machine.

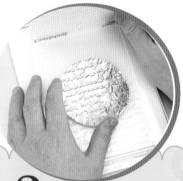

3 Remove the embossed circle from the plate.

LOOK FOR INTERESTING EMBELLISHMENTS

I am sure when they made these cute little name tags I found in a bin at the dollar store, they never dreamed they would end up on a scrapbook page! My son has had many names over the years, so as soon as I saw these drink markers lined up in the packaging, I knew exactly how I wanted to use them. Because they were intended for use on glass, I ran them through an adhesive machine so they would adhere to the page and make the perfect accent for this page theme.

Supplies

Cardstock; patterned paper (BasicGrey, Cosmo Cricket); alphabet stickers (Sassafras Lass, American Crafts, Making Memories); asterisk sticker (Sassafras Lass); name tags (Dollar Tree); ribbon (Offray); brads (Karen Foster Design); Misc: binder clip

Make It Fabulous!

When you have a non-time-specific page theme, try choosing photos that span several years to indicate time passing within the page theme.

30-45 MINUTES

Here is the proof that I'm living vicariously through my sister! I am so happy she finally had a cute little girl so I could buy yummy vintage-style dresses like this one. It was hard for me to imagine not ever having a daughter, but sweet Lily is a perfect addition to my life

the dress

Lily Belle 4/08

INCORPORATE INEXPENSIVE PAPER DOILIES

Because she only has boys, Shannon is enjoying buying cute little dresses like this one for her niece. She wanted to create a pretty, feminine page. What could be more feminine than a doily? She created a border by cutting out the zigzag pattern of the paper and added flowers, butterflies and pink scalloped ribbon to really turn up the girl volume! The doily adds a perfect spot for journaling, and for only pennies, Shannon got just the feminine touch she was looking for.

Supplies

Patterned paper, felt stickers (K&Company); doily (unknown); ric rack (Wrights); felt ribbon (Creative Imaginations); crown note sheet (Heidi Swapp); pink bobby pin (Pebbles); magical digital sparkles (in photo background) (Anna Aspnes for Designer Digitals); Misc: pen, foam adhesive; font: Bettyshand

PAGE BY SHANNON TAYLOR

45-60 MINUTES

Where do we go to escape the 98 degree weather of Utah summers? We go to Grandpa Sumerix's house of course. He has a gorgeous elm tree in his front yard that completely shades us while the kids run through the sprinkler and we all eat a picnic. We find ourselves looking for excuses to go and visit whenever we're feeling the heat of summer.

PAGE BY JEN GALLACHER

30-45 MINUTES

WASH WOODEN TAGS WITH WATERED-DOWN ACRYLIC PAINT

Jen was so excited to find this tree paper to scrapbook about the large tree in her dad's yard. A picnic under the tree provided the perfect photos to use with the paper. The washed effect on the wooden tags is a subtle and easy technique that doesn't distract from her adorable son. Wooden tags are inexpensive and can be stained any color in the rainbow with acrylic paint.

Supplies

Cardstock; patterned paper (KI Memories, Chatterbox); tags (Craft Supply); ribbon (Offray); chipboard letters (Scenic Route); Misc: brown photo corners, circle punch, corner rounder punch; font: 2Peas Tubby

materials

ACRYLIC PAINT, WATER, PAINTBRUSH, WOODEN TAGS, PAPER TOWEL

1 Mix a small amount of acrylic paint with water.

2 Use a paintbrush to apply the paint to a tag.

3 Wipe off any excess paint with a paper towel.

CUT IT UP

Cutting out patterns from what you already have is a great way to save some money. Look for products and items that can pull double duty if they are cut apart.

CUT YOUR TITLE FROM A PHOTO

Materials for titles can add up quickly, so when I see a chance to create a cost-effective title, I take it! I snapped this picture of the restaurant sign where we were eating and thought it would make a great page title. I printed a 5 x 7 (12.7cm x 17.8cm) copy of the photo and, using a craft knife, cut directly around the image. (See inset photo.) Take pictures of signs or images that could be cut out and used as titles on your layouts.

Supplies

Cardstock; patterned paper (The Paper Studio, DCWV, Scenic Route); palm tree sticker (K&Company); date sticker (EK Success); ribbon (The Paper Studio); rub-ons (American Crafts, K&Company); Misc: circle punch, corner punch, micron pen, ink

30-45 MINUTES

Up & down, up & down is how the story goes. But watch yourself, try to be safe or land upon your nose. Jump high & low, try to be seen, nothing's more fun that a trampoline!

CUT EMBELLISHMENTS FROM PATTERNED PAPERS

PAGE BY
SHANNON TAYLOR

These photos of her son jumping up and down on the trampoline are some of Shannon's favorites! She wanted to simulate that motion on her layout, so she chose chevron patterned papers and cut out different colors, patterns and widths. Overlapping the strips of this zigzag pattern gave just the feeling of movement Shannon was looking for. She used foam adhesive behind some of the strips for dimension and then hand stitched the same up-and-down pattern over the cut strips for texture and interest. Look for patterns in your paper that can be used as embellishments that highlight your photo subjects or themes.

Supplies

Patterned paper (Cosmo Cricket); arrow rub-on (Polar Bear Press); letter stickers (Making Memories, K&Company); metal edge tags (Making Memories); twine (Pebbles); chipboard frame (SEI); Misc: foam adhesive, font: Impossibilium

60-90 MINUTES

CHAPTER FOUR

FABULOUS LAYOUT DESIGN

You can have all the latest products and the best of intentions, but if you don't have a layout design, you can't scrapbook. I am a total sketcher. I can't remember the last time I made a page without making a quick sketch first. I use graph paper so my sketches will be to scale, and I keep them in a pad so I can flip through and find them or remove them and put them in a notebook. I sketch at night before I go to bed, when I am waiting on my kids in the pick-up line at school—any time I have a few extra minutes.

As an art teacher, my work centers on the elements and principles of design, and I incorporate these into my scrapbook pages. By focusing on design and sketching out my ideas, I can sit down when I have a few minutes to scrap and can create with confidence because the prep work is done and all the design questions have already been answered. In this chapter, I share not only my sketches with you but also design principles and hints to make every page you create fast, fun, frugal and fabulous!

FLIP YOUR SKETCH

The best thing about having sketches to work from is that they provide a blue-print that can be changed and used over and over again. Take a look at these lay-outs made from the same sketch.

GO BIG TO SAVE TIME

Although I like being in the creek as much as the next person, only a boy could see the fun in kissing a slimy salamander! Yuck! Using large elements, like the 5 x 7 (12.7cm x 17.8cm) photo, a block of tan cardstock and a premade license plate, helps create this striking design in a matter of minutes.
To bring balance to the layout and move the eye in all directions, I combined the vertical lines of the license plate and title with the horizontal lines of the cardstock block and supporting photos.

Supplies

Cardstock (Prism); patterned paper (Scenic Route); license plate connector (Keller's Creations cut from Reminisce); chipboard ring (Imagination Project); alphabet stickers (American Crafts); ribbon (Offray); Misc: binder clips

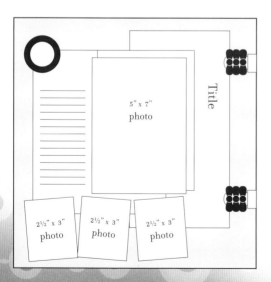

Make It Fast!

Make quick work of your journaling by printing key words associated with the pho-tos onto coordinating strips. Add a small alphabet sticker as the first letter of a few of the words to add color and interest.

SMiLE

A glimpse of who you are

Sometimes my taking your picture is not really your idea of fun. As I took these photos of you by the pond, the time between each shot was spent with you whining about how hot it was, how you didn't want to be there and how you wished I would hurry. You did still manage to put on a happy face each time I snapped a picture. I just love to see you smile...even when I know the dark truth behind it!

30-45 MINUTES

SCRAPLIFT YOURSELF

Once you have a great design, use it again! You've already done the work; just change it up a bit for a totally different look. By rotating the *All Boy* sketch one quarter turn, I have a whole new design without investing any more time or effort. Like the *All Boy* layout, I used the license plate and large cardstock block but added more embellishments with punched and sticker flowers for a more feminine look. Note that one of the smaller photos has been substituted with a die cut block and flower accents. If you look at each element in your design as if it can be replaced with something completely different, you can recycle your designs over and over again without anyone being the wiser.

Supplies

Cardstock; patterned paper (Karen Foster Design); license plate connector (Keller's Creations cut from Reminisce); velvet stickers, chipboard ring (EK Success); die cut letters, quote (Daisy D's); ribbons (American Crafts); Misc: flower punch

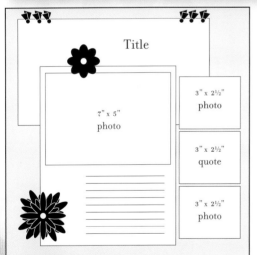

Title

7" x 5"
photo

3" x 2½"
photo

3" x 2½"
quote

3" x 2½"
photo

Make It Frugal!

Create inexpensive embellishments by punching from paper scraps like I did with the layered flowers on this page.

CALL ATTENTION TO A FOCAL POINT

A focal point is the element of your page that you view to be the most important or one of the most important parts of your layout. Try these ideas to highlight your focal points.

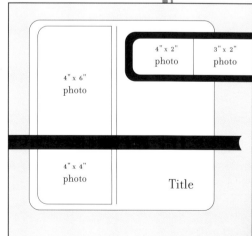

30-45 MINUTES

ZOOM IN AND CROP

I fell in love with these pictures my father took while docked during a cruise. My dad didn't have a macro lens, so the original photos appeared as if they were taken from far away. I used my photo editing program to zoom in on the caterpillars and cropped the photos, eliminating the distracting background and pulling all the focus to the caterpillars. Their bright colors were the basis for the green-and-yellow color scheme, and the little fuschia flowers in one of the photos inspired my accent color.

Supplies

Cardstock; patterned paper (Piggy Tales); flowers (Prima); brads (Karen Foster Design, Making Memories, The Paper Studio); rhinestone flowers (Petaloo); chipboard slide (Colorbök); chipboard alphabet (Heidi Swapp); ric rack border (Doodlebug Design); ribbon (Michaels); Misc: safety pin

PHOTOS BY PAUL KETRON

JUL 03 2008

I got Jimmy and Katelyn up early so that we could go and watch
the Freedom Festival Balloon launch. I love
the sound of the firing up of the balloons and then
watching them ascend into the air. So peaceful and magical!

balloon launch

15-30 MINUTES

PAGE BY JEN GALLACHER

SHOW OFF A LARGE PHOTO

When you have a great photo, show it off! Jen printed her photo as an 10 x 8 (25.4cm x 20.3cm) and then cropped it to 10 x 5 (25.4cm x 12.7cm) to leave room for the other two photos. By printing them as 5 x 3.5 (12.7cm x 8.9cm), they were the exact width of the larger photo. Her simple accents and title keep the focus of the layout on the photos. Jen used strips of paper behind her title for her journaling, which separated her photos, followed the horizontal line of the photos and provided continuity to the layout.

Supplies

Cardstock; patterned paper (KI Memories); acetate stars (Heidi Swapp); alphabet stickers (Doodlebug Design); corrugated oval die cut (Déjà Views); buttons (American Crafts); twine (Craft Supply); Misc: date stamp; font: 2Peas Hot Chocolate

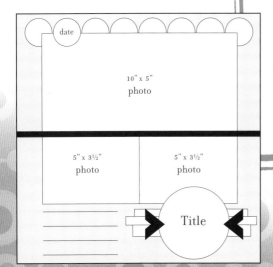

SPECIMEN

BUG.

Date: 2006 Time: Summer
Location: Back yard
Notes:
"I don't think this one is a Lady Bug... it looks more like a teenager bug" — shianne age 7

FOR OFFICIAL USE ONLY
Shi anne W.

USE TO COLLECT COMMON OR UNCOMMON BITS OF LIFE:
FINGERPRINTS, A KISS, BUG SHOTS, WHATEVER

15-30
MINUTES

**PAGE BY
SHAUNTE WADLEY**

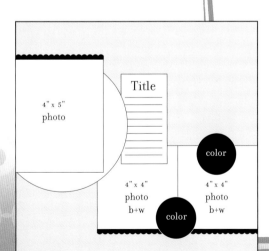

4" x 5"
photo

Title

4" x 4"
photo
b+w

color

color

4" x 4"
photo
b+w

FAKE A COOL DIGITAL TRICK
TO EMPHASIZE A FOCAL POINT

I hate to admit it, but I am not digitally savvy. I love the look of digitally coloring black-and-white photos, so when I saw Shaunte's fake-out, I knew it was a trick I was going to try. She printed her photos in color and then converted them to black-and-white and printed them again. She punched the ladybug image out of the color photos and, after cropping her black-and-white pictures, she overlaid the color circles to match the images and emphasized them with rings. Notice that the colored circles extend slightly past the edge of the black-and-white photos, making the ladybug stand out even more.

Supplies

Patterned paper (Scenic Route, Creative Imaginations, BoBunny); tag (7gypsies); scrapper's floss (Karen Foster Design); circle cutter (EK Success); Misc: ink

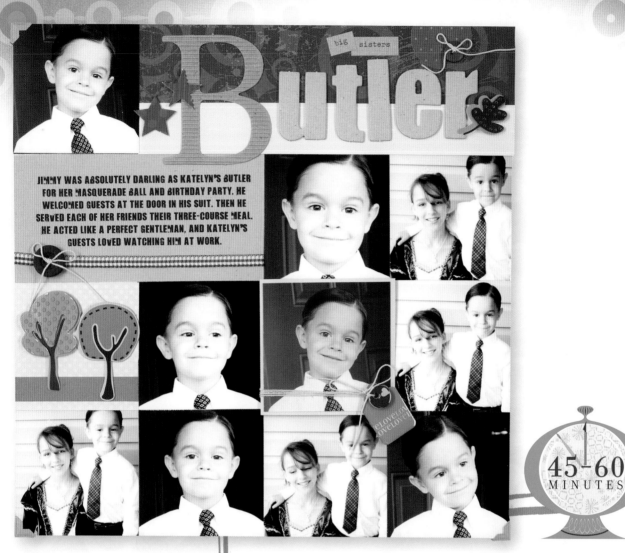

PAGE BY JEN GALLACHER

PRINT A STANDOUT PHOTO IN COLOR

Who wouldn't love to have this adorable little butler waiting on them hand and foot? Jen captured this moment at her daughter's party with a series of photos of the little butler and his "boss." When you have a number of quality photos on your layout, you can help make the best one stand out by printing it in color and printing the rest in black-and-white. Once Jen printed her focal photo in color, she also matted it in blue and used twine to add a cute little tag for extra emphasis. Even with the multiple photos on this layout, your eye is immediately drawn to the precious smile in the color photo.

Supplies

Patterned paper (Little Yellow Bicycle, Sassafras Lass, BoBunny, KI Memories); corrugated cardstock (Déjà Views); chipboard stars, word stickers, heart and love tags (Making Memories); buttons (American Crafts, BasicGrey); twine (Craft Supply); leaf and tree stickers (Target); ribbon (Offray); Misc: circle punch; font: Uptown

3" x 3" b + w	Title		
		subtitle	
		3" x 3" b + w	3" x 3" b + w
3" x 3" b + w	3" x 3" b + w	3" x 3" color	3" x 3" b + w
3" x 3" b + w	3" x 3" b + w	3" x 3" b + w	3" x 3" b + w

45–60 MINUTES

CROP AND FRAME A NOT-SO-PERFECT PHOTO

We all have those photos that we love but that just aren't the best quality. I really wanted to use this sweet picture of the kiss, but it was a little out of focus and didn't look as good as the other photos. I eliminated a lot of the focus problems by cropping the photo. I helped distract from its quality by placing it in this colorful chipboard frame and adding the accent word.

Supplies

Patterned paper (BasicGrey, BoBunny, Karen Foster Design); flocked alphabet stickers (EK Success); alphabet stickers (Colorbök); rub-ons (BasicGrey); chipboard accents (Miss Elizabeth's); twill (Autumn Leaves); brads (Karen Foster Design); Misc: ink

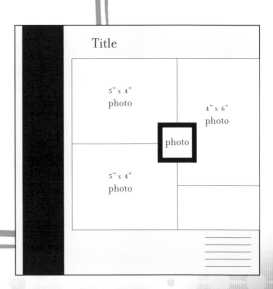

45-60 MINUTES

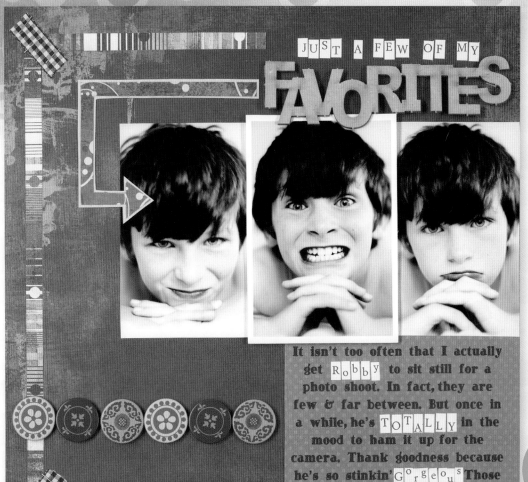

JUST A FEW OF MY

FAVORITES

It isn't too often that I actually get Robby to sit still for a photo shoot. In fact, they are few & far between. But once in a while, he's TOTALLY in the mood to ham it up for the camera. Thank goodness because he's so stinkin' Gorgeous! Those teeth, those eyes, that hair, that pale skin! Absolute Perfection

45-60
MINUTES

PAGE BY SHANNON TAYLOR

DRAW ATTENTION TO YOUR PHOTOS WITH AN ARROW

I hate to state the obvious, but the focus of every layout should be the photos. What better way to draw attention to the focus of the page than by pointing directly to it? The arrow in this layout leaves no doubt where the focal point is, and these fantastic photos deserve all the attention it brings to them. I agree with Shannon—her son is gorgeous!

Supplies

Patterned papers (BasicGrey); alphabet stickers (Making Memories); chipboard title (Creek Bank Creations); large brads (SEI); ribbon (Fancy Pants Designs); Misc: staples, font: Ding Dong Daddy O

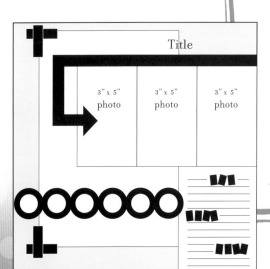

Make It Fabulous!

Arrows come in all shapes and sizes. In addition to calling attention to pictures as a whole, they can be used to point out particular items or areas within the photos.

TITLE DESIGN

Titles can really draw attention to your layouts, and coming up with a great title design is sometimes difficult. Use these ideas to make easy work of great titles.

30-45 MINUTES

MAKE YOUR TITLE POP

Shaunte's take on this sketch is so cute! I love the way she took the idea of the oversized letter and switched it up to a large chipboard flower in place of the *A* in her title. Either way, making one part of your title different from the rest adds interest and gives you a standout element for your layout. The rhinestone circle helps bring the two parts of the title together. Shaunte repeated the circle on her focal photo to tie the title into the rest of the layout.

Supplies

Patterned paper, chipboard flower, transparent floral accent (Fancy Pants Designs); chipboard title, scallops (Creek Bank Creations); rhinestone circles (Best Occasions)

PAGE BY SHAUNTE WADLEY

Make It Fast!

Bare chipboard, like the title on this layout, looks cool, and using it as is saves you the time of painting, ink-ing or covering it.

Darcie is one well dressed dog!

Sometimes she doesn't mind

a well tailored jacket or a T.....   but forget the costumes!

October   2008

45–60 MINUTES

ADD A ROUND TITLE TO A HORIZONTAL LAYOUT

Believe it or not, Darcy doesn't mind getting dressed up at all—as long as it doesn't involve her head! These photos look great together, but the layout needed something to break up the horizontal lines created by both the photos and the mat. To solve this problem, I added a patterned paper circle behind the title for contrast. Using the dotted paper, ribbon and round rhinestone accent, I tied the circle into the remainder of the page.

Supplies

Cardstock; patterned paper (BoBunny); chipboard title and accents (Creek Bank Creations); ribbon (American Crafts, May Arts); rhinestone (Darice); Misc: photo corners, ink

Title

subtitle

All the kids have a favorite kind of apple.

Of course they aren't all the same, so we

end up buying three different kinds.

Thank goodness for the variety bag!

45–60 MINUTES

STAMP A TEXTURED PATTERN

I love creating my own embellishments, but I also want the process to be quick and easy like these stamped, hand-cut images. Acrylic stamps come in so many different patterns that the possibilities for textures with this technique are endless. I freehand drew the apples on this page, but if you can't draw, you can always punch an image or even trace a template and cut it out.

Supplies

Cardstock; scalloped cardstock (DCWV); acrylic stamps (Keller's Creations); alphabet stickers (American Crafts); ribbon (Michaels, The Paper Studio); Misc: paint samples, buttons, ink

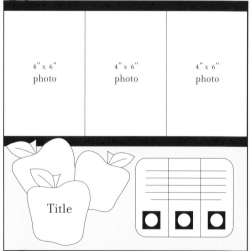

materials

ACRYLIC STAMPS, FOAM BRUSH, ACRYLIC
PAINT, CARDSTOCK, WATERMARK INK,
PENCIL, SCISSORS

1 Paint an acrylic stamp with a foam brush and acrylic paint.

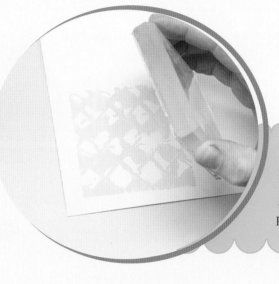

2 Stamp on cardstock. Repeat the process with the watermark ink.

3 Draw your desired image on the stamped paper and cut it out.

LOAD ON THE PHOTOS

One way to save time and money and showcase all your fabulous photos is to follow designs that accommodate as many pictures as possible. These sketches hold tons of photos while leaving room for your artistic abilities to shine.

PILE ON THE PHOTOS

When you have a subject as cute as Shannon's niece, you can't help but take tons of photos! To accommodate more of them, skip the mats and pile on the photos just like Shannon did in this layout. She was able to fit seven pictures on this page and still have room for some great chipboard accents. Journaling on strips that run the width of the page and placing them above and below the photos keeps the layout clean and simple and moves the eye back and forth over the photos.

Supplies

Textured cardstock (Bazzill Basics); patterned paper, crown die cut, chipboard accents (Fancy Pants Designs); alphabet stamps (All Night Media); Misc: foam adhesive; font: Claritta Bold Italic

PAGE BY SHANNON TAYLOR

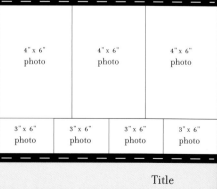

45-60 MINUTES

TAKE A SKETCH AND MAKE IT YOUR OWN

One of the best things about sketches is that they are just a starting point. I came up with this sketch, and Shaunte totally made it her own. While she kept the small photos, strips of paper and rings, she moved the title and subtitle, and it looks great! Shaunte skipped the journaling altogether because the photos are portraits of her immediate family. These changes look great and are a wonderful example of altering a sketch to meet your needs.

Supplies

Textured cardstock (Bazzill Basics); patterned paper, chipboard accents, brads (BasicGrey); die cut alphabet letters (QuicKutz); circle cutter (EK Success)

PAGE BY SHAUNTE WADLEY

CREATE A LACY SCALLOPED BORDER

Color blocking photos and patterned paper on one large mat is a quick and easy way to create a layout. With the time I saved color blocking on this layout, I created this easy border from a precut scalloped page. This sketch accommodates up to nine photos along with the handmade border accent. The title, journaling, photos or patterned paper can be moved to any square you like, making this layout completely versatile to meet your specific needs.

Supplies

Cardstock; patterned paper, chipboard letters, button, ribbon, foam accent (American Crafts); scalloped border (Bazzill Basics); Misc: hole punch

Title	3" x 3" photo	3" x 3" photo	
	3" x 3" photo	3" x 3" photo	
		3" x 3" photo	

A trip to Cades Cove was such an exciting thing after living away from East Tennessee for a year and a half. This day we got to see a bear on top of our usual wildlife of deer and birds. Our family is so grateful to be living near our family and friends in East Tennessee.

materials

SCALLOPED PAPER, PAPER TRIMMER, TWO SIZES OF HOLE PUNCH, RIBBON, EMBELLISHMENT

1 Cut a 2" (5.1cm) edge from a precut scalloped page.

2 Punch a hole in the middle of each scallop. Use a smaller hole punch to punch on either side of the middle hole for a lace effect.

3 Add ribbon and embellishments to the scalloped strip.

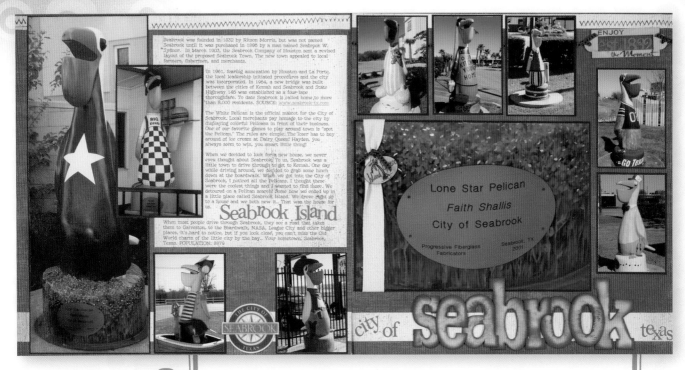

FIT MULTIPLE PHOTOS AND LENGTHY JOURNALING

You don't have to make a choice between numerous photos and lengthy journaling, as Julie's layout shows. With careful planning, she was able to incorporate ten photos and still tell the story of her favorite landmarks in her hometown. She even downloaded and printed the city seal to use on her page. This layout means even more to Julie since Hurricane Ike destroyed many landmarks in her beloved city.

Supplies

Patterned paper (Daisy D's); alphabet stickers (Chatterbox); wooden accents (Go West Studios); cardstock letters (Gin-X); ribbon (Making Memories); fabric accent (Li'l Davis Designs); twill (Wrights); Misc: ink

PAGE BY JULIE JOHNSON

60–90 MINUTES

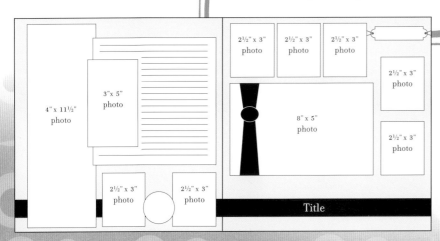

overlap your photos

One speedy way to accommodate photos is to overlap them. These designs show you ways to overlap without losing any impact.

PHOTOS BY RENEE NICOLO

USE EMBELLISHMENTS TO CONNECT PHOTOS

Placing photos where they touch or overlap each other, like the middle and lower photos on this layout, moves the eye from one photo to the next. A curved line of buttons ties the middle and upper photos together to make one continuous curve for the eye to follow between all three photos.

Supplies

Cardstock; patterned paper (The Paper Studio, Foof-A-La); chipboard letters (EK Success); ribbon (Foof-A-La); white pen (Uni-ball); Misc: acrylic paint, ink

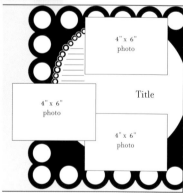

45-60 MINUTES

Siblings forever & always! I can tell he will always look after her! Lily + Eli

60-90 MINUTES

PAGE BY
SHANNON TAYLOR

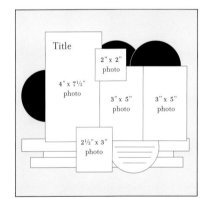

Title

2" x 2" photo

4" x 7½" photo

3" x 5" photo

3" x 5" photo

2½" x 3" photo

OVERLAP PHOTOS TO FIT MORE ON THE PAGE

How sweet are these adorable water babies? Shannon loved how these pictures turned out and wanted to use as many of the shots as possible. To maximize the number of photos on the page, Shannon placed some of the smaller pictures on top of the larger ones. You don't want to cover up essential parts of your photos, but don't be afraid to overlap photos in dead space. Placing the title on her largest photo also gave Shannon room for more photos on the remainder of the page.

Supplies

Patterned papers, flower clips, ribbon (KI Memories); Misc: pen, acrylic paint, foam adhesive

Make It Frugal!

Try painting a large mat around all of your photos with acrylic paint like Shannon did. It acts as a border for all the photos and adds a punch of color for mere pennies.

Be Design Savvy

Little design tricks and great layouts can make your scrapbooking more eye appealing. Try these design ideas to make quick work of layouts that will make you proud.

DOUBLE THE DIFFERENCE

This sketch is a great example of the "double the difference" trick I learned when matting children's artwork for art shows. Artwork is most visually pleasing when there is more space below the focal point than above it. If you take the area above your photos and double it, then you have the amount of space that will be most visually pleasing below the photos. The colorful squares in the patterned paper made it easy to place the photos in this manner by leaving one row showing above and two showing below.

Supplies

Cardstock; patterned paper, rub-ons (American Crafts, Creative Imaginations); ribbon (American Crafts); alphabet and number stickers (Making Memories); Misc: circle punches

PHOTOS BY NAN EVANS

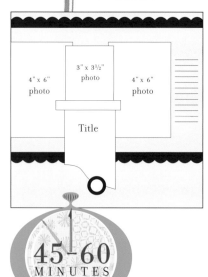

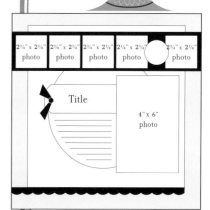

USE PRODUCT LINES TO ENSURE A COHESIVE LOOK

Does this go? I hear that question over and over, from my kids picking out their clothes to my scrapbooking friends trying to decide what products to use. Picking products for layouts is always a challenge, so why not let the manufacturer do all the work for you? Many companies produce all-inclusive lines with paper, stickers, rub-ons, alphabets, ribbons and more, all designed to work together. Purchasing a full or partial line of products takes the guesswork out of the matching dilemma and gives you the ability to create several pages guaranteed to look great!

Supplies

Cardstock; patterned paper (Fancy Pants Designs, My Mind's Eye); chipboard alphabet, rub-ons, die cuts (Fancy Pants Designs); tag (Avery); Misc: ink

ALEX SURPRISED US AT CHRISTMAS WITH GORGEOUS PHOTOS OF ALL THE CHILDREN

30-45 MINUTES

TRY A VERSATILE DESIGN

You can use up to eight photos on this layout, or you can follow the design and use patterned paper or even journaling in some of the 3" x 4" (7.6cm x 10.2cm) spaces; it is up to you and your needs. I love this design for series photos or pictures from the same photo shoot because they can be placed side by side and look cohesive with no need for mats to separate them. A quick change of papers and embellishments makes this layout adaptable for any theme or photos.

PHOTOS BY RENEE NICOLO

Supplies

Patterned paper (My Mind's Eye, BasicGrey, Doodlebug Design); alphabet stickers, metal circle tags, epoxy stickers (EK Success); ribbon (Crafts, Etc!); rub-ons (Sassafras Lass); chipboard bird (Magistical Memories); brads (Karen Foster Design); label maker (DYMO); Misc: ink, buttons, staples, flower punches, circle punch

Title			
3" x 4" photo		3" x 4" photo	3" x 4" photo
	3" x 4" photo	3" x 4" photo	

Make It Fabulous!

Since the page design divides the layout into thirds horizontally with two-thirds being photos and one-third being title and journaling, the layout has a balanced design and is visually pleasing.

114

15-30
MINUTES

LANdon   Ashley   NaThan

10/31/08

JOURNALING NOT REQUIRED

Although scrapbooking is all about recording photos and the story behind them, not every layout requires journaling. On this Halloween layout, it is obvious from the photos and the title that the children are trick-or-treating. All I needed to add was their names and the year. When something special, funny or sentimental happens, you definitely want to find the time and space to journal about it. Sometimes the photos tell the story already, so don't feel bad for not journaling on all your pages!

PHOTOS BY
ALANA TURNER

Supplies

Cardstock; patterned paper (My Mind's Eye, PineCone Press); connectors (Keller's Creations cut from Pinecone Press); alphabet stickers (American Crafts, Doodlebug Design, The Paper Loft); turns, brads (The Paper Studio); ribbon (Making Memories); Misc: staples, ink

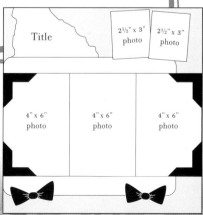

CREATE WITH COLOR

Choosing colors can be confusing, so let the color wheel be your guide to make easy work of this process.

CREATE A COMPLEMENTARY COLOR SCHEME

Complementary color schemes feature two colors that are exact opposites on the color wheel. This layout of my son learning to ride a bike consists of the complements blue and orange. Other complementary color schemes include red and green, yellow and violet—any two colors that are directly across from each other on the color wheel. Complementary colors are guaranteed to look good together.

Supplies

Patterned paper, chipboard letters, alphabet die cuts (The Paper Loft); precut rings (Keller's Creations); number stickers (Karen Foster Design); white pen (Uni-ball); Misc: circle punches, acrylic paint, ink

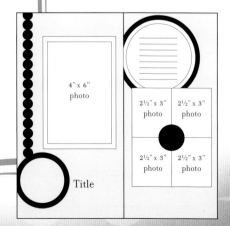

out with anna

Every day,
Any day,
going on
an outing
with
Anna is a
hilarious,
crazy, loud, wild adventure.
I wouldn't have it any other
way!
~2008

15-30 MINUTES

PAGE BY
SHANNON TAYLOR

TRY A TRIADIC COLOR SCHEME

Triadic color schemes consist of three colors that are equal distances apart from each other on the color wheel. Shannon's gorgeous layout uses the triad of violet, green and orange. You can find a triadic color scheme by starting with a primary, secondary or tertiary color on the color wheel. Count four colors over from the original color and then four more. This will give you a triadic color scheme and three colors that look great together. The other triads on the color wheel are yellow, blue and red; blue-violet, red-orange and yellow-green; and blue-green, yellow-orange and red-violet.

Supplies

Patterned papers (Making Memories); alphabet stickers (Chatterbox); chipboard arrow (Sandylion); silk flowers (Prima); ribbon (Wal-Mart); Misc: pen, buttons

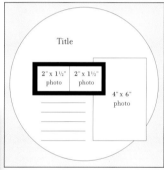

Title

2" x 1½" photo 2" x 1½" photo

4" x 6" photo

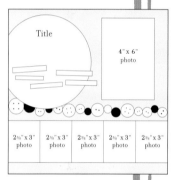

Title

4" x 6" photo

2⅜" x 3" photo 2⅜" x 3" photo 2⅜" x 3" photo 2⅜" x 3" photo 2⅜" x 3" photo

MASTER A MONOCHROMATIC COLOR SCHEME

I just adore these pictures of Ashleigh in the garden. My layout of this bean-picking trip was a perfect page for a monochromatic green color scheme. Monochromatic color schemes are made up of various shades and tints of one color, plus black and white. When you are using only one color, remember to use a variety of shades to keep your layout interesting. The addition of black rub-ons and white accents adds contrast to a layout that is all one color.

Supplies

Cardstock; patterned paper (BoBunny, Karen Foster Design); chipboard letters (DCWV, EK Success, Making Memories); paper flowers (Target); felt flowers (American Crafts); rub-ons (The Paper Studio); season sticker (Karen Foster Design); ribbon (Offray); Misc: buttons, ink, acrylic paint

BEANS

Ashleigh had such a great time picking beans at Uncle Jimmy and Aunt Oneida's. She picked, froze and even cooked her beans!

Summer

45-60 MINUTES

PHOTOS BY
ALANA TURNER

SHAPE UP YOUR LAYOUTS

Use shape to support your layout theme and draw your eye around the page.

USE A SHAPE TO SUPPORT A THEME

When I was taking these pictures for my daughter, I thought, "She has a great circle of friends." That thought led to every aspect of this layout, from the title to the embellishments. The ring within the scalloped circle draws the eye in a circle around the page, from the title to the journaling around the photos and back to the title. Circular embellishments like buttons, brads and hole reinforcers all support the layout theme.

Supplies

Patterned paper (Pink Paislee, Jenni Bowlin); alphabet stickers (EK Success, American Crafts, Doodlebug Design); brads (The Paper Studio); Misc: hole reinforcers, buttons, ink

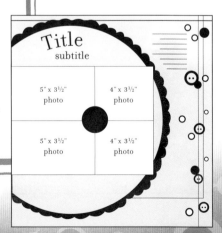

Swimming is always one of the things the boys look forward to in the summertime every year.

USE SHAPE TO CREATE MOTION

45-60 MINUTES

Shape can create a sense of motion like the chipboard wave on this swim lesson layout. To further emphasize the wave motion, I mounted the photos to cardstock, traced the chipboard wave across the bottom and cut along the line. Matching the wave pattern of the chipboard accent increases the sense of movement and helps the eye follow the photos across the page. Try using a wave pattern for beach photos, backyard water play or even sports fan photos. (The wave, get it?)

Supplies

Patterned paper (Fancy Pants Designs); chipboard title, wave (Creek Bank Creations); chipboard accent (Miss Elizabeth's); rub-ons (American Crafts); circle brads (The Paper Studio); acrylic stamps (Keller's Creations, Studio G); ribbon (American Crafts, Offray); chain (Leisure Arts); Misc: binder clip, acrylic paint, buttons, ink

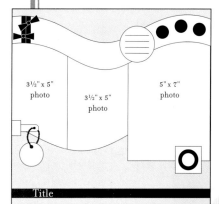

3½" x 5" photo

3½" x 5" photo

5" x 7" photo

Title

DESIGN YOUR EMBELLISHMENTS

It is always fun to make something totally different and amazing from things you already have. Try these techniques to design fabulous embellishments for your pages.

30-45 MINUTES

PULL AN ELEMENT FROM THE PHOTOS TO SIMULATE AN EMBELLISHMENT

Holy cow! When my boys shoved their heads through the fence to get a better look at the alligator in the water below, I could just envision all the bad things that could happen. I quickly tried to look at it from a scrapbooker's point of view instead of as a mom. I climbed onto the fence to get a shot of them from above and snagged a really cool focal photo. I loved the way the marsh moss looked on the water and used the mesh to give that same feel to the page. Cutting it in uneven strips and staining the edges with dark ink gives it the look of moss and makes a perfect accent for this gator-themed page.

Supplies

Patterned paper (The Paper Loft, Dream Street Papers); mesh (Magic Mesh); alphabet stickers, ribbon (American Crafts); chipboard element (Heidi Swapp); label tape (DYMO); Misc: chalk ink, acrylic paint, buttons

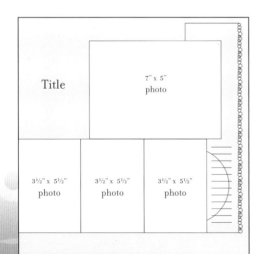

2001 - 2005

Hayden is all boy from head to toe!

He is mischievious, rough, and has a

mean streak a mile long!

But he can also be sweet and loving

and he is just so darn cute!

my BOY

30–45 MINUTES

CREATE A LEATHER-LOOK ACCENT WITH CHIPBOARD AND FAUX FINISH PAINT

My son is all boy from head to toe, and I wanted that to come across in my layout. Because the photos were all headshots, I wanted to bring the mischievous-boy feel to my page through my embellishments and title. What says "boy" more than leather? This faux leather finish can be used on any chipboard element or letter. The blue-and-brown color scheme and the inked chipboard barbed wire added to the masculine feel of this simple sketch.

Supplies

Patterned paper (BasicGrey, The Paper Loft); chipboard letters, barbed wire (Creek Bank Creations); chipboard tag (The Paper Studio); alphabet stickers (American Crafts); suede paint, fixative (Krylon); Misc: ink

4" x 6" photo   4" x 6" photo   4" x 6" photo

Title

materials
CHIPBOARD TAG, MAKE IT SUEDE PAINT, CHALK INK, FIXATIVE

1 Spray the chipboard with Make It Suede paint and let the paint dry (15–20 minutes).

2 Ink the edges and surface lightly with chalk ink.

3 Spray with fixative to seal.

contributing artists

jennifer gallacher

I have worked as a designer, teacher and writer for the scrapbooking industry for ten years now. I have loved designing for companies such as Making Memories, Li'l Davis Designs, Little Yellow Bicycle, CreativeXpress, Inque Boutique and Karen Foster Design. In addition to design team work, I enjoy creating for a variety of scrapbooking magazines and have had many projects published through the years. When I'm not designing a scrapbook page, project or card, I'm probably writing a scrapbooking article or reading one. My husband and I have two children and currently live in Utah. Outside of the scrapbooking world, I love playing the piano and am passionate about decorating.

julie johnson

I am a stay-at-home mom to my son, Hayden, and love every minute of it! I live in Seabrook, Texas, with Hayden and my wonderful husband, Darrell. They are my favorite subjects to scrapbook. I have worked on design teams for Queen & Co., Krylon and EK Success. I have been scrapbooking for six years and was honored when named a 2005 Memory Makers Master. In addition, I have been published in numerous magazines and books, but love just scrapbooking for myself! When I am not scrapbooking, I love to be outside on and in the water and traveling with my family.

sHannon TaYLor

I live in a comfortable cottage overrun by my two beautiful boys (Robby and Oliver), hunky husband (Rob) and happy hound dog (Auggie Doggy). I attempt a girly existence in the midst of sports and camouflage by surfing scrapbook sites on my pink computer, chatting with friends on my pink phone and watching romantic movies (not on a pink TV). I happily split my time between a part-time graphic designer job and my full-time mother position. I make bright, colorful, happy scrapbook pages that have been seen in numerous magazines and idea books over the last six years. I feel blessed to have won two national scrapbooking contests, including being named a 2005 Memory Makers Master. The only thing I need is for my siblings to continue producing nieces and nephews so I can scrap forever.

sHaunte WaDLey

I am a thirty-something, caffeine-addicted, chocolate-loving, SAHM (stay-at-home mom) from Utah. I have been scrapbooking since 1997, the dreaded era of photos cropped with deco scissors. Since then, my work has evolved into a clean, lin-ear, photo-focused style. I have been published a few times, been to a few trade shows, taught a few classes, worked for a few design teams—but have not yet lost the love for this hobby. I love it for the creative outlet and the good people I have met along the way.

My favorite subjects are my husband and five kids (I never lack for subject material). I especially like making mini-albums of our many trips together. When I'm not scrapping, I am blog hopping, reading or editing photo shoots. And doing laundry. Always laundry.

source guide

The following companies manufacture products featured in this book. Please check your local retailers to find these materials, or go to a company's Web site for the latest product. In addition, we have made every attempt to properly credit the items mentioned in this book. We apologize to any company that we have listed incorrectly, and we would appreciate hearing from you.

3M
(888) 364-3577
WWW.3M.COM

7GYPSIES
(877) 749-7797
WWW.SEVENGYPSIES.COM

ALEENE'S - SEE DUNCAN ENTERPRISES

ALL NIGHT MEDIA—SEE PLAID ENTERPRISES

ALL STUCK UP

AMERICAN CRAFTS
(801) 226-0747
WWW.AMERICANCRAFTS.COM

AMERICAN GREETINGS

AMERICAN TRADITIONAL DESIGNS/MOMENTA
(800) 448-6656
WWW.AMERICANTRADITIONAL.COM

AROUND THE BLOCK
(801) 737-9197
WWW.AROUNDTHEBLOCKPRODUCTS.COM

ART WAREHOUSE

ARTISTIC SCRAPPER—NO SOURCE AVAILABLE

ARTISTIC WIRE, LTD.
(630) 530-7567
WWW.ARTISTICWIRE.COM

AUTUMN LEAVES / CREATIVITY, INC.
WWW.AUTUMNLEAVES.COM

AVERY DENNISON CORP.
(800) 462-8379
WWW.AVERY.COM

BASICGREY
(801) 544-1116
WWW.BASICGREY.COM

BAZZILL BASICS PAPER
(800) 560-1610
WWW.BAZZILLBASICS.COM

BERWICK OFFRAY, LLC
(800) 237-9425
WWW.OFFRAY.COM

BEST OCCASIONS

BOBUNNY PRESS
(801) 771-4010
WWW.BOBUNNY.COM

CHARTWELL STUDIO, INC.

CHATTERBOX, INC.
(877) 749-7797
WWW.CHATTERBOXINC.COM

CHERRYARTE
(212) 465-3495
WWW.CHERRYARTE.COM

CLEARSNAP, INC.
(888) 448-4862
WWW.CLEARSNAP.COM

COLORBÖK, INC.
WWW.COLORBOK.COM

CORE'DINATIONS
WWW.COREDINATIONS.COM

COSMO CRICKET
(800) 852-8810
WWW.COSMOCRICKET.COM

CRAFT SUPPLY

CRAFTS, ETC!—SEE STAMPABILITIES

CREATE-A-CRAFT

CREATIVE IMAGINATIONS
WWW.CIGIFT.COM

CREATIVE MEMORIES
(800) 468-9335
WWW.CREATIVEMEMORIES.COM

CREEK BANK CREATIONS, INC.
(217) 548-2132
WWW.CREEKBANKCREATIONS.COM

DAISY BUCKET DESIGNS
(541) 289-3299
WWW.DAISYBUCKETDESIGNS.COM

DAISY D'S PAPER COMPANY
(888) 285-7575
WWW.DAISYDSPAPER.COM

DARICE, INC.
(866) 432-7423
WWW.DARICE.COM

DCWV (DIE CUTS WITH A VIEW)

DÈJÁ VIEWS/C-THRU RULER
(800) 243-0303
WWW.DEJAVIEWS.COM

DELTA CREATIVE, INC.
(800) 423-4135
WWW.DELTACREATIVE.COM

DESIGNER DIGITALS
WWW.DESIGNERDIGITALS.COM

DMC CORP.
(973) 589-0606
WWW.DMC-USA.COM

DOLLAR TREE

DOODLEBUG DESIGN, INC.
(877) 800-9190
WWW.DOODLEBUG.WS

DREAM STREET PAPERS
(480) 275-9736
WWW.DREAMSTREETPAPERS.COM

DUNCAN ENTERPRISES
(800) 438-6226
WWW.DUNCANCERAMICS.COM

DYMO
(800) 426-7827
WWW.DYMO.COM

EK SUCCESS, LTD.
WWW.EKSUCCESS.COM

EVERLASTING KEEPSAKES
(816) 896-7037
WWW.EVERLASTINGKEEPSAKES.COM

FANCY PANTS DESIGNS, LLC
(801) 779-3212
WWW.FANCYPANTSDESIGNS.COM

FAVORITE FINDINGS

FIBERS BY THE YARD
WWW.FIBERSBYTHEYARD.COM

FLORACRAFT
WWW.FLORACRAFT.COM

FOOF-A-LA

GILL MECHANICAL COMPANY

GIN-X

GO WEST STUDIOS
WWW.GOWESTSTUDIOS.COM

GREENBRIER INTERNATIONAL

HALLMARK CARDS, INC.
(800) 425-5627
WWW.HALLMARK.COM

HEIDI SWAPP/ADVANTUS CORP.
(904) 482-0092
WWW.HEIDISWAPP.COM

HERO ARTS RUBBER STAMPS, INC.
WWW.HEROARTS.COM

HOBBY LOBBY STORES, INC.
WWW.HOBBYLOBBY.COM

IMAGINATION PROJECT—NO LONGER IN BUSINESS

IMAGINISCE
(801) 908-8111
WWW.IMAGINISCE.COM

JENNI BOWLIN
WWW.JENNIBOWLIN.COM

JO-ANN STORES
WWW.JOANN.COM

JUDIKINS
(310) 515-1115
WWW.JUDIKINS.COM

JUNKITZ - NO LONGER IN BUSINESS

K&COMPANY
(800) 794-5866
WWW.KANDCOMPANY.COM

KAREN FOSTER DESIGN
(801) 451-9779
WWW.KARENFOSTERDESIGN.COM

KELLER'S CREATIONS
(229) 226-0800
WWW.ACIDFREE.COM

KI Memories
(972) 243-5595
WWW.KIMEMORIES.COM

Krylon
(800) 457-9566
WWW.KRYLON.COM

Leisure Arts/Memories in the Making
WWW.LEISUREARTS.COM

Li'l Davis Designs

Little Yellow Bicycle

Magic Mesh
(651) 345-6374
WWW.MAGICMESH.COM

Magic Scraps - no longer in business

Magistical Memories
(818) 842-1540
WWW.MAGISTICALMEMORIES.COM

Magnetic Poetry
(800) 370-7697
WWW.MAGNETICPOETRY.COM

Making Memories
(801) 294-0430
WWW.MAKINGMEMORIES.COM

Martha Stewart Crafts
WWW.MARTHASTEWARTCRAFTS.COM

Marvy Uchida/ Uchida of America Corp.
(800) 541-5877
WWW.MARVY.COM

May Arts
WWW.MAYARTS.COM

Maya Road, LLC
(877) 427-7764
WWW.MAYAROAD.COM

Me & My Big Ideas
(949) 583-2065
WWW.MEANDMYBIGIDEAS.COM

Michaels Arts & Crafts
WWW.MICHAELS.COM

Miss Elizabeth's - no source available

MMBI

My Mind's Eye, Inc.
(801) 298-3709
WWW.MYMINDSEYE.COM

October Afternoon
(866) 513-5553
WWW.OCTOBERAFTERNOON.COM

Offray—see Berwick Offray, LLC

Pageframe Designs
(435) 864-4006
WWW.PAGEFRAMEDESIGNS.COM

Paper Company, The
(800) 449-1125
WWW.PAPERCOMPANY.COM

Paper Loft, The
(801) 254-1961
WWW.PAPERLOFT.COM

Paper Studio, The
(480) 557-5700
WWW.PAPERSTUDIO.COM

Paperbilities - no source available

Pebbles, Inc.
(800) 438-8153
WWW.PEBBLESINC.COM

Petaloo
(818) 707-1330
WWW.PETALOO.COM

Piggy Tales
(702) 755-8600
WWW.PIGGYTALES.COM

Pinecone Press
(714) 434-9881

Pink Paislee
WWW.PINKPAISLEE.COM

Plaid Enterprises, Inc.
(800) 842-4197
WWW.PLAIDONLINE.COM

Polar Bear Press - no source available

Pressed Petals
(801) 224-6766
WWW.PRESSEDPETALS.COM

Prima Marketing, Inc.
(909) 627-5532
WWW.PRIMAMARKETINGINC.COM

Prism
(866) 902-1002
WWW.PRISMPAPERS.COM

Provo Craft
(800) 937-7686
WWW.PROVOCRAFT.COM

PSX Design
WWW.SIERRA-ENTERPRISES.COM/PSXMAIN.HTML

Queen & Co.
(858) 613-7858
WWW.QUEENANDCOMPANY.COM

QuicKutz, Inc.
(888) 702-1146
WWW.QUICKUTZ.COM

Reminisce Papers
WWW.SHOPREMINISCE.COM

Rubber Soul
(360) 779-7757
HTTP://RUBBERSOUL.MYSHOPIFY.COM

Sandylion Sticker Designs
(800) 387-4215
WWW.SANDYLION.COM

Sassafras Lass
(801) 269-1331
WWW.SASSAFRASLASS.COM

Scenic Route Paper Co.
(801) 653-1319
WWW.SCENICROUTEPAPER.COM

ScrapVillage
WWW.SCRAPVILLAGE.COM

Scribble Scrabble
(801) 400-9741
WWW.SCRIBBLESCRABBLE.NET

SEI, Inc.
(800) 333-3279
WWW.SHOPSEI.COM

Sonburn, Inc.
(800) 436-4919
WWW.SONBURN.COM

Stampabilities/Crafts, Etc!
(800) 888-0321
WWW.STAMPABILITIES.COM
WWW.CRAFTSETC.COM

Streamline

Studio G

Sulyn Industries, Inc.
WWW.SULYN.COM

Target
WWW.TARGET.COM

Teresa Collins

Teters Floral Products Inc.
(800) 999-5996
WWW.TETERS.COM

Therm O Web, Inc.
(800) 323-0799
WWW.THERMOWEB.COM

Two Peas in a Bucket
(888) 896-7327
WWW.TWOPEASINABUCKET.COM

Uni-ball/Sanford
(800) 323-0749
WWW.UNIBALL-NA.COM

Wal-Mart Stores, Inc.
WWW.WALMART.COM

We R Memory Keepers, Inc.
(801) 539-5000
WWW.WERONTHENET.COM

Winsor & Newton
(800) 445-4278
WWW.WINSORNEWTON.COM

Wordsworth - see Rubber Soul

Wrights Ribbon Accents
(877) 597-4448
WWW.WRIGHTS.COM

index

Make your scrapbooks even more fast, fun, frugal and fabulous with these other fine Memory Makers titles.

THE BUSY SCRAPPER

You can scrap fast and hassle-free! Packed with tips and techniques showing you how to scrap in a flash, this book is a one-stop guide to efficient layouts that are fun to make.

ISBN-13: 978-1-59963-029-8
ISBN-10: 1-59963-029-X
paperback
128 pages
Z2141

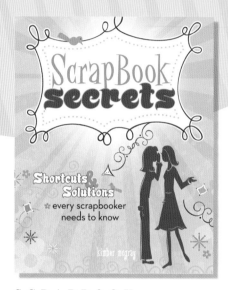

SCRAPBOOK SECRETS

Get the scoop on 50 simple secrets that will help you scrap better, scrap faster and have fun along the way.

ISBN-13: 978-1-59963-034-2
ISBN-10: 1-59963-034-6
paperback
128 pages
Z2460

GET IT SCRAPPED!

Author and artist Debbie Hodge offers her unique methodology for creating several common page types in this must-have resource for getting layouts done.

ISBN-13: 978-1-59963-015-1
ISBN-10: 1-59963-015-X
paperback
128 pages
Z1597

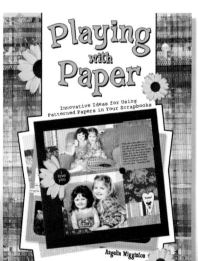

PLAYING WITH PAPER

Have fun playing with paper with ideas for mixing patterns in a wide variety of ways. Includes step-by-step instructions for creative but simple paper techniques.

ISBN-13: 978-1-59963-033-5
ISBN-10: 1-59963-033-8
Paperback
128 pages
Z2390

These books and other fine Memory Makers titles are available at your local scrapbook retailer, bookstore or from online suppliers. Or visit our Web site at www.mycraftivitystore.com.